UCI

Bright Past, Brilliant Future

UCI

Bright Past, Brilliant Future

Sharon L. Roan + John Westcott

EDITED BY Marina Dundjerski

UC Irvine: Bright Past, Brilliant Future
© 2015 The Regents of the University of California

First published in 2015 by Third Millennium, an imprint of
Profile Books Ltd., in conjunction with UC Irvine.

Irvine, CA · London

Third Millennium
3 Holford Yard, Bevin Way
London, WC1X 9HD, United Kingdom
www.tmiltd.com

UC Irvine
Office of the Chancellor
500 Aldrich Hall
Irvine, CA 92697-1075

ISBN: 978 1 908990 23 5

Library of Congress Control Number: 2014957252

Edited by Marina Dundjerski
Principal photography by Julian Andrews
Jacket design by Jennie M. Brewton
Layout design by Matthew Wilson
Production by Debbie Wayment
Proofreading by Kymberly Doucette and Neil Burkey

Reprographics by Studio Fasoli, Italy
Printed and bound in China by 1010 Printing International Limited
on acid free paper from sustainable forestry.

Set in TheSerif on 95lb/140gsm matte art

THIRD MILLENNIUM
PUBLISHING, LONDON

contents

foreword

"Bright past, brilliant future." What a perfect description of UC Irvine and its Anteater family.

The campus has established itself as a provider of first-class educational and extracurricular experiences for a diverse student body and as a premier research institution. Notably, it is a focal point for the thriving cultural and business community that surrounds it, thanks to the impact made by students, faculty, staff and alumni. UCI develops the doctors and nurses, the lawyers and leaders, the educators, artists, inventors and business executives of tomorrow. It embraces the bold and independent thinking that often changes the world.

Perhaps no one demonstrated that ethic so profoundly—and so early in UCI's history—as F. Sherwood Rowland, the Nobel Prize laureate in chemistry. He saw that a byproduct of aerosol sprays was destroying the ozone layer and became the rare scientist to actively advocate a ban on consumer products. He saw truth, acted on his convictions, and won.

As UCI begins its next 50 years, that spirit is inspiring innovative advances in knowledge. Collaborative research centers convening bright minds from across the campus tackle current issues, starting with water resource management, health and wellness models, and the wide role of data in academic endeavors. Campus leaders forge partnerships with venture capitalists to help guide and fund student, faculty and alumni entrepreneurs. Technology incubators nurture start-up companies fueled by academic research. Community college students pair up with UCI's engineering students to learn desktop manufacturing techniques, a program that answers the calls for increased US productivity and seamlessness within California's education system. And these are just a few examples.

We look forward with optimism to the brilliant future UC Irvine will build—is building even now—on the strong foundation of its bright past.

Congratulations, Anteaters.

Janet Napolitano
President, University of California

chapter 1

ranch of
destiny

William Pereira, whose thoughtful designs gave birth
to UC Irvine and the metropolis that surrounds it, knew
his blueprints weren't etched in stone. They would—and
should—continue to evolve long after he moved on.

"If 100 years from now, the Irvine campus and its community
still look as we picture them in our master plan, we shall have in
a sense failed," he told NBC as the first structures awaited their

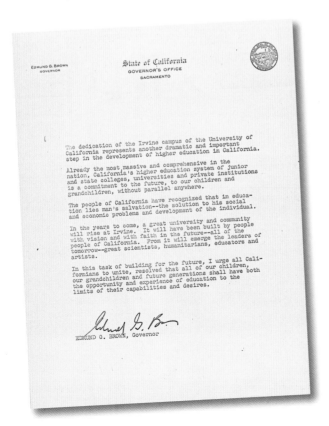

State of California
GOVERNOR'S OFFICE
SACRAMENTO

EDMUND G. BROWN
GOVERNOR

The dedication of the Irvine campus of the University of
California represents another dramatic and important
step in the development of higher education in California.

Already the most massive and comprehensive in the
nation, California's higher education system of junior
and state colleges, universities and private institutions
is a commitment to the future, to our children and
grandchildren, without parallel anywhere.

The people of California have recognized that in education lies man's salvation--the solution to his social
and economic problems and development of the individual.

In the years to come, a great university and community
will rise at Irvine. It will have been built by people
with vision and with faith in the future--all of the
people of California. From it will emerge the leaders of
tomorrow--great scientists, humanitarians, educators and
artists.

In this task of building for the future, I urge all Cali-
fornians to unite, resolved that all of our children,
our grandchildren and future generations shall have both
the opportunity and experience of education to the
limits of their capabilities and desires.

EDMUND G. BROWN, Governor

▶ With uncanny similarity to the flag-raising at Iwo
Jima, workmen plant one of the campus's first trees
near the Library-Administration building (renamed
Jack Langson Library on October 16, 2003, after a gift
from the Newport Beach entrepreneur).

◀ Governor G. Edmund "Pat" Brown congratulates the
campus on its dedication: "In the years to come, a
great university and community will rise at Irvine."

A Presidential Dedication

More than 15,000 people gathered on a sparse field on June 20, 1964, to hear President Lyndon B. Johnson dedicate the University of California, Irvine.

Many drove or walked down the narrow two-lane dirt road that connected the site with the outside world. The campus, a work in progress, wouldn't open for another 15 months. But that didn't stop the president and other dignitaries—including Governor Edmund G. "Pat" Brown, UC President Clark Kerr and founding chancellor Daniel G. Aldrich Jr.—from setting expectations for the newest UC campus and its future students and faculty.

"All our hopes depend on the kind of society we can build in the United States," Johnson said during his brief remarks that focused on educational policy. "That in turn rests on our system of education. I do not intend for us to settle for an easy peace for the world—an inferior society for America—or an adequate education for our children. We are on the frontiers of a new America. Ahead of us is the challenge to make our system work in a dangerous and difficult period."

Said Brown, who noted that California's population made it the largest state in the nation: "We face the greatest demand for higher education that has ever been known in the history of mankind. ... Education has made California great, and will make her greater."

occupants. "But if generations hence, this campus and city are capable of being physically altered by needs we know nothing of now, and if all the while the university and the city of Irvine are a vital and dynamic force in an unfamiliar new world of the future, we shall have succeeded beyond our fondest dreams."

Pereira couldn't foresee the exact twists and turns that UC Irvine's development would take, but perhaps it did succeed beyond his and others' "fondest dreams." The first half-century saw a dedication and commencement address by two sitting presidents, three Nobel Prizes go to campus faculty, membership in the elite Association of American Universities (of which UC

Irvine is the youngest), and a ranking in 2014 as first in the nation among universities less than 50 years old, as judged by *Times Higher Education* magazine of London.

It all started long before Pereira made his first pencil marks on paper, with an idyllic ranch populated by more deer and jackrabbits than people.

> "Irvine is not conceived as an isolated academia but as an institution that plays an active role in the transfer of learning to life."
>
> —Daniel G. Aldrich Jr.
> FOUNDING CHANCELLOR

▲ *President Lyndon B. Johnson surprises his Secret Service detail by moving into the crowd at the conclusion of the site dedication, June 20, 1964.*

◄ *Founding Chancellor Daniel G. Aldrich Jr. presents the Chain of Title to President Johnson.*

▶ *Chet Huntley of NBC News talks with Chancellor Aldrich minutes before filming a scene for the documentary, 1,000-Acre Campus, January 12, 1964.*

◀ *An original Irvine Ranch building, just a few hundred yards away from the heart of campus.*

"ONE OF THE GREAT BARGAINS OF ALL TIME"

What *was* the Irvine Ranch, birthplace of UC Irvine? It once was one of the two largest private ranches in America, sprawling over a third of Orange County. Centuries before, it was wilderness speckled with small Tongva (or Gabrielino) villages, followed by a patchwork of Spanish and then Mexican ranchos. Mostly, it was grazing land for sheep and cattle. After the Mexican War of the 1840s, Americans gradually took over the ranchos, aided by the bad weather, lawsuits and crushing debt that forced three rancheros to sell their land to three American sheep ranchers. One, a Scotch-Irishman named James Irvine, bought out his partners four years later. The result: a massive ranch that stretched 23 miles from the Pacific Ocean north to the Santa Ana River, 110,000 acres in all.

His son, James Irvine Jr., inherited this huge landmass. "J.I." was like his dad; he enjoyed owning a ranch, but preferred urban San Francisco. It took the devastating 1906 earthquake to change his mind. Irvine pulled up stakes and moved south, growing to love the rugged, peaceful land. He took long horseback rides to survey his domain, and hunted and fished when he wasn't inspecting crops or worrying about finances.

Parts of the ranch found unexpected uses throughout the years. The Buffalo Ranch started with more than 70 bison shipped in from Kansas, and featured burgers and a trading post run by Chief Push Ma-Ta-Ha. Fascinated by science and technology, Irvine offered a landing field for Orange County's first airplane, which was assembled in an abandoned church by a young Santa Ana man (and future aircraft entrepreneur) named Glenn L. Martin. Irvine eagerly hitched a ride into the sky. America's first Nobel Prize laureate in the sciences, Albert A. Michelson, later built a mile-long vacuum tube across a bean field and measured the speed of light. Even then, this was a land for science and innovation.

> "It was a world of cowboys and farmers. We had lunch with all the ranch hands."
>
> —Barbara Gray
>
> RESEARCH ASSISTANT FOR ARCHITECT WILLIAM PEREIRA, RECALLING THE DAYS OF MEETING AT THE UCI OFFICE AT THE IRVINE RANCH HOUSE, ACROSS IRVINE BOULEVARD AND NEAR THE IRVINE COMPANY'S AGRICULTURAL HEADQUARTERS

▼ *Joan Irvine Smith (left) with her mother, Athalie Clarke, c. 1964.*

Mostly, the ranch was put to agricultural use: grazing land for sheep, then cattle; tidy rows of olive, orange and lemon trees. Lima bean fields stretched so far, the ranch was rightfully called "the lima bean capital of the world"—until the best fields were commandeered by the US government to accommodate warplanes at the new El Toro Marine Corps Air Station. Soon, another corner of the ranch was taken, this time to house blimps used as Pacific Coast sentries at another military base, in today's Tustin. America was at war, so Irvine did his duty. But it fueled a bitter distrust of government. He vowed his land would never willingly be sold for public purposes—even after his death, in 1947 at the age of 80.

The rules for charitable giving by the James Irvine Foundation included this stipulation: No gifts would ever go to tax-supported institutions. Period. The foundation had a 51 percent controlling interest in decisions by the Irvine Company. The stipulation became the biggest obstacle when the University of California came calling in 1959, after Irvine's son and heir, Myford "Mike" Irvine, died. The university needed lots of land to build on for the projected wave of young people expected to nearly double the number of eligible students over the next decade.

Clark Kerr, who had taken the reins as UC president two years earlier, made finding room for this oncoming "tidal wave" his top priority. Under the state's new Master Plan for Higher Education of 1960—which guaranteed "educational access for all"—three new University of California campuses were placed on the assembly line. Newly hired Pereira drew up a list of 21 possible sites on the sparsely populated landscapes of southeast Los Angeles County and Orange County.

The list was trimmed to five, including one inside the Irvine Ranch. Development had nibbled at the edges of the ranch over the years, but it still sprawled 93,000 acres. Kerr liked the Irvine site. He believed its vast expanse of empty land, all held by a single owner, would make the complex job of building a large campus much simpler.

But not *that* simple. Arthur J. McFadden, elevated to Irvine Company president after Mike Irvine died, argued that a wealthy, tax-supported institution like the University of California didn't need the foundation's charity, despite the university's insistence on a donation. Joan Irvine Smith, J.I.'s granddaughter, disagreed. She was Joan Irvine Burt then, and a regular thorn in the side of McFadden and other trustees. She often filed lawsuits as a negotiating tool.

March 1959 *UC Board of Regents authorizes William Pereira to begin campus planning*

September 30, 1960 *The Irvine Company sells 1,000 acres for $1; later, the UC buys 510 additional acres*

January 19, 1962 *Daniel G. Aldrich Jr. appointed chancellor*

December 13, 1962 *Regents approve Pereira's architectural plans and select him to create campus master plan*

1963 *Town and Gown established*

September 6, 1963 *Pereira and his work planning UC Irvine and the city of Irvine make cover of* Time *magazine*

1964 *First buildings open: the Interim Office Building and the Faculty Research Facility*

June 20, 1964 *President Lyndon B. Johnson dedicates the campus*

July 1965 *Friends of UCI incorporated*

September 26, 1965 *First student-faculty convocation held in Campus Hall*

Chain of Title, documenting the deed transfer from the Irvine Company to the Regents of the University of California, recorded January 20, 1961. Abiding by James Irvine's restriction that no assets be donated to a public institution, the land "sold" for $1.

▼ Marker at exact geographical hub of the campus.

"Plato said that the beginning is the most important part of the work, and today an auspicious beginning is being made."

—Clark Kerr
UNIVERSITY OF CALIFORNIA PRESIDENT, 1958–1967

Her friend Walter Burroughs, publisher of the *Daily Pilot* newspaper for Newport Beach and Costa Mesa, urged her to support a community effort to bring the university to the ranch. Irvine Burt immediately saw the advantages, knowing what UCLA did for Westwood years earlier. Burroughs and his friend Brick Powers amassed a following of 50,000 residents to help lobby for a campus. Negotiations began moving smoothly toward an offer of 650 acres of Irvine Ranch land.

If that offer had manifested, UC Irvine would now be in Newport Beach. It would overlook the harbor, in a spot later known as Spyglass Hill. During negotiations, however, the Irvine Company sold part of the site to Pacific View Memorial Park—a cemetery. Irvine Burt offered another site to the cemetery, but Pacific View was happy where it was—and the issue became moot after several bodies were buried there. UC Irvine had to go somewhere else.

Fortunately, another site emerged. It was 5 miles inland, a 650-acre spot called the San Joaquin foothills. Pereira pronounced it just as majestic as the first choice. Irvine Burt pushed the board to increase the donation to 1,000 acres and it was approved on a telephone vote. To get around James Irvine Jr.'s restriction against donating assets to a public institution, the land was "sold" for $1. Technically, it was a "friendly condemnation," not a donation. Either way, it was a deal that Donald Cameron, an urban planner who worked for Pereira, would describe as "one of the great bargains of all time."

In September 1960, the Irvine Company formally transferred the site to the University of California. A few years later, after more negotiation, the company sold the university 510 additional acres, called an "inclusion" area. The campus was coming to Irvine.

The visionary

Pereira never did anything halfway. While searching for possible sites for the new UC campus, he didn't just pore over maps and tour the best prospects. He haunted the campuses of Harvard and Yale and studied universities in France, Italy and Scotland. He read voraciously, consulting the ancient Greeks on what made a university site special. His conclusion: The best sites are able "to create a contemplative mood, to stimulate thought and to inspire invention." They must offer a "sense of place." Just as important, a great campus needs space to grow and a supportive community.

Pereira already had a reputation for futuristic designs. He had developed the master plan for the 1933 Chicago World's Fair. Later, he drew up iconic designs for Los Angeles International Airport and Marineland of the Pacific on the Palos Verdes Peninsula. Before he was done, he designed the famous Transamerica Pyramid in San Francisco. Over his career, he crafted an astonishing 400 buildings. But nothing compared to what he was asked to do in Irvine: create a university and, later, the city around it, from scratch.

He housed his team of planners in an old red barn—left over from the Buffalo Ranch—he dubbed Urbanus Square. The result was the notable, if not mellifluously named, "Second Phase Report for a University-Community Development in Orange County." The work also took an exhaustive look at the city to grow around UC Irvine. His 10,000-acre vision called for a town of at least 50,000 residents, including 15,000 students. It featured light industry, shopping areas and acres of greenbelts. The Irvine Company was so impressed it asked Pereira to draw up a master plan for the entire Irvine Ranch.

Time magazine put him on its cover in September 1963. In the article, Pereira predicted a world in which people walked to work and to shop. "While the auto was supposedly freeing the individual and his family from the asphalt jungles, our open spaces have been overpowered in much the same manner that the tropical jungle eventually mastered the great cities of the Yucatán," he said. "Take parking lots. A great deal of open land has been withdrawn to provide parking lots. Nothing is more ugly."

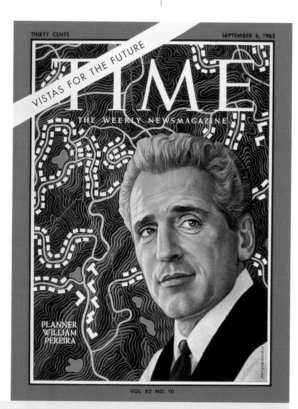

> *"The university will be a real link between town and gown, a place intimately connected with the center of learning."*
>
> —William Pereira
> *Time, September 6, 1963*

Daniel G. Aldrich Jr.

Chancellor 1962–1984

Grand vision and attention to detail distinguished The University of California, Irvine's founding chancellor, Daniel G. Aldrich Jr. He spent three years forming an interdisciplinary university. For the next 19 years, he would stop midstride to pluck a candy wrapper from the walkway or pull an offending weed from the landscaping of his beloved campus.

Humble, cultured, described by the UC Regents as "a man whose values are as rock-ribbed and solid as the hills of his native New England," Aldrich led the university for a record-setting 22 years. He fought for free speech, defending faculty and students who invited Black Panther leader Eldridge Cleaver to speak on campus. He recruited top-notch, pioneering faculty. He was sensitive to the local community, which was initially suspicious of the university. When his decade-long quest to build a campus hospital threatened UC Irvine's relationship with its neighbors, he conceded.

In an early documentary, Aldrich described his vision: "We expect Irvine to take its place among the great general campuses of the University of California, and those students who go forth from here shall have received an education of quality, of character and diversity that will enable them to respond appropriately wherever they may find themselves."

After retirement, Aldrich battled colon cancer with the same determination he employed in all his endeavors. During a remission, Aldrich—an avid athlete in javelin, discus, hammer throw and shot put—medaled in international competition.

Jack W. Peltason, who succeeded Aldrich as chancellor, told the *Los Angeles Times* after Aldrich's 1990 death, "His memorial is all around us: it is UCI."

He got most of his greenbelts. But parking lots were inevitable, although parts of the campus were closed off to cars. Overall, his vision endured, recalled Ray L. Watson, who worked closely with Pereira as head planner for the Irvine Company.

"Bill Pereira, to me, is the real visionary," Watson, who served as president of the Irvine Company from 1973–1977, told the *Orange County Register* years later. "He is the person who convinced the company, who convinced the university, to do this university city. Without that vision, without that salesmanship, I don't think this ever would have happened."

▲ *Aldrich, UC Irvine's first chief executive, led the campus for an unprecedented 22 years.*

▼ *Founders' Rock, in Aldrich Park, honors the founding chancellor with words by architect William Pereira: "The right man came at the right time, and from the bare ground built a place as lasting."*

THE FOUNDING CHANCELLOR

The first two times Clark Kerr asked, Daniel G. Aldrich Jr. said no. But the University of California president was convinced that Aldrich was the man to lead UC Irvine, so Kerr kept asking. Aldrich was a soils scientist and prided himself on improving the lives of thousands of farmers. After leading departments at UC Davis and UC Berkeley, he was dean of agriculture for the UC system. He told Kerr it was "the best job in the world." Why would he leave it?

Slowly, Aldrich warmed to the idea of starting a campus from scratch. He saw it as the modern version of the land-grant system he had studied at the University of Rhode Island, focusing on environmental planning and community service. On December 6, 1961, Kerr asked a third time, and Aldrich finally said yes. The path for the rest of Aldrich's life was set: He was a founding chancellor.

▼ *From left, Aldrich, Charles S. Thomas (Irvine Company president from 1960–1966) and Pereira at architects' headquarters at Urbanus Square.*

▲ *Standing from left, Regent Donald H. McLaughlin, Regent Gerald H. Hagar, Irvine Company President Charles S. Thomas, and seated from left, Aldrich, Regent Dorothy B. Chandler and UC President Clark Kerr, during an official visit to campus.*

From left, Aldrich with Jack W. Peltason, vice chancellor of academic affairs; Richard L. Balch, vice chancellor of student affairs; and Edward A. Steinhaus, dean of the biological sciences; check out campus progress. Aldrich made key hires to help build a comprehensive university—and gain a strong academic reputation—from the start.

▼ *L.E. Cox, vice chancellor for business and finance, and UC Irvine's first employee, manages the $30 million campus construction.*

> *"How do you start a new university? The median age of professors then was about 30. Some ideas worked, some didn't."*
>
> —Michael Burton
> ANTHROPOLOGY PROFESSOR SINCE 1969

At one point, Aldrich brought daughter Liz, then 16, to the UC Irvine site. "Can you see what I'm looking at?" he asked. She couldn't; all she saw was endless brown dirt and rocks. But she could tell that her father saw much more: a shiny new campus sprouting from the ground. "He was given an opportunity that really very few are given—to make something out of nothing," she recalled. "He could see it all."

With barely more than three years before the campus opened, Aldrich immersed himself in the planning process. One day he and William Pereira walked past a rocky outcropping. That should be the central point, Aldrich said. Pereira made it so. The park that someday would bear Aldrich's name was born as Campus Park.

The chancellor assembled a team to help him run the campus; some he knew, others were recommended. Aldrich's first hire was L.E. Cox, as vice chancellor of business and finance. He was followed by Ivan Hinderaker, a UCLA political science professor who began work on the academic plan and, as the first vice chancellor of academic affairs lined up deans and department chairs. Other early choices included Edward A. Steinhaus, considered the father of modern invertebrate pathology, to lead the biological sciences division; Ralph W. Gerard, already a member of the National Academy of Sciences as an authority on brain function; and Jack W. Peltason, a specialist in American government known admiringly as "The Wonder Boy."

Aldrich and the others worked to tie the young campus to the community. His wife, Jean, joined with Frosty Gerard, wife of Ralph, to form Town and Gown, which included both faculty wives and women from the Newport Beach and Costa Mesa areas. (There was no city of Irvine yet.) The group began with 500 members that first year, peaking later at more than 1,000.

Looking south from Mesa Court: the Commons (renamed Gateway Study Center) and just behind it, Library-Administration, October 1966.

▼ *Connie Sunblad and Janice Jenkins of student affairs mail the first 1965–1966 catalogs.*

▶ *First day of classes, October 4, 1965.*

"The future belongs to our youth."
—Inaugural yearbook editors

Aldrich was determined that UC Irvine open as a comprehensive university. He had seen campuses such as UC Davis, at first only an agricultural station, have a difficult time getting the respect and attention they deserved. People couldn't see past the limited beginnings. He refused to let that happen to UC Irvine.

The new chancellor promised to look at academia through fresh eyes, allowing faculty to organize their departments unburdened by old ideas. The new social ecology department—the first of its kind in the nation—was an amalgam of urban planning, development and transportation, but also of law enforcement, ethnic issues, healthcare and prisons. Its professors asked such questions as: What helps to create a healthy human ecology?

"He consulted with everyone," said Robert Cohen, who jumped at the chance to leave Yale University to head the drama department. "He didn't just run over people." Clayton Garrison, the first dean of fine arts, broke from the tradition of stressing theory, putting the emphasis on performance. "It was very new, very fresh at UC Irvine," Cohen said.

He himself liked to push the envelope on what a university performance could be, though once he feared he'd pushed too far. He staged the play *Equus* with a seduction scene in which performers took their clothes off. When he glimpsed Aldrich, a devout Christian, among the opening-night crowd, Cohen feared the worst. "But at the end, he walks up to me and says, 'Robert, that was the best show I've ever seen.'" Cohen recalled. "I was so relieved. I wasn't going to lose my job."

The campus opened on October 4, 1965, with 1,589 students. Each had been urged ahead of time to read *The Aims of Education*, by Alfred North Whitehead, to get them in the spirit of helping usher in the new campus. The inner core of eight buildings had been completed. The bookstore, a Bank of

April 20, 1967 UCI acquires California College of Medicine

October 2, 1967 UCI Faculty Club opens

November 6, 1967 UCI Foundation incorporated

1968 Edward A. Steinhaus is first UCI professor elected to National Academy of Sciences

September 23, 1968 New University *student newspaper begins publication (previous incarnations included* The Spectrum, *first published in October 1965)*

1969 Men's swim and dive team wins first of three consecutive NCAA championships

January 14, 1969 Campus Hall gymnasium-auditorium renamed Crawford Hall after first athletic director Wayne Crawford

▲ *Early Anteater logos.*

America branch and a post office sat in temporary trailers across the street. The campus employed 119 faculty, 43 teaching assistants and 241 additional staff.

With bulldozers and heavy equipment crawling around, greenery had to wait. Students tramped their way to class the first year through kicked-up dust or sticky mud, depending on the weather.

Aldrich made himself visible and accessible. He talked with students, staff and faculty. He wanted to hear their thoughts and concerns. In an era of student uprising, demonstrations at UC Irvine were generally peaceful. Many credited Aldrich's style of calm engagement and listening to complaints.

For the most part, Aldrich allowed faculty and students to forge the campus's beginnings. The Academic Senate wrestled with many of the big issues, such as setting UC Irvine's academic structure, voting "no" to bringing in football and "no" again to introducing fraternities and sororities, though Greek organizations would arrive later. Aldrich gave the same freedom to students. When they voted down traditional mascot names like "Seahawks" in favor of the quirky, iconoclastic "Anteater," Aldrich wasn't happy, but he bit his tongue.

◄ *Students Dale Finney and Barbara Terhune and the El Toro US Marine Corps Color Guard raise the Stars and Stripes at Anteater Plaza for the first time, September 14, 1965.*

21

October 21, 1969 KUCI debuts on air with Problems of the World Solved Tonight

November 1969 Regents buy San Joaquin Marsh

1970 Farm School founded (moves to Aliso Viejo in 2013); social ecology founded

January 1970 TRIGA Mark I nuclear reactor installed

September 1970 Coed living introduced in Mesa Court

November 6, 1970 University Orchestra premieres in Village Concert Hall

November 28, 1970 Men's water polo wins UCI's first NCAA University Division title

1971 Men's tennis wins second consecutive NCAA championship (Division II)

December 28, 1971 Irvine residents vote to incorporate as a city

1972 Conquest of the Planet of the Apes filmed on campus

October 30, 1972 Thesaurus Linguae Graecae holds first planning conference

1973 Men's baseball and men's tennis win NCAA championships

1974 Baseball team wins second consecutive NCAA title

Spring 1974 Rush held for inaugural sororities (Delta Gamma, Pi Beta Thi and Gamma Phi Beta) and fraternities (Beta Theta Pi, Phi Delta Theta and Sigma Chi)

May 1974 Women's tennis wins Southern California Championship

September 1974 Middle Earth residence hall, named for J.R.R. Tolkien's mythical land, opens for 350 students

▶ *Commencement ceremonies in Campus Park, June 14, 1969.*

Excitement, growth and innovation defined UCI's early years. The campus unexpectedly acquired the California College of Medicine, though some faculty were concerned it was too soon. Nevertheless, it became the campus's first professional school. By fall 1969, enrollment reached 5,024. Many felt the campus was on its way to achieving its full projected enrollment of 27,500 by 1980. Then reality got in the way.

TOUGH TIMES CALL FOR A PRIVATE APPROACH

The 1970s dawned amid controversy. Kerr was ousted by Governor Ronald Reagan and replaced by new UC President Charles J. Hitch, who announced that the 1950s projections that had called for three new UC campuses—Irvine, San Diego and Santa Cruz—had been vastly overstated. The news was a shock. Instead of shooting for 27,500 students, UC Irvine was asked to settle for 7,500. It was later raised to 9,000.

The action "suggested that we were going to have to completely undo that which we had planned and were headed toward," Aldrich told founding dean of the School of Humanities and UCI historian Samuel Clyde McCulloch in 1989. The 1970s provided a period of retrenchment and meager budgets under Hitch and his successor, David S. Saxon; UC Irvine's landscape welcomed only a single new building as the university's rapid growth ground to a halt.

The 1980s began with an unpromising recession that further pinched Sacramento's resources, but fortunes for the young campus were about to change. In 1983, Aldrich found a sympathetic ear to his pleas for more money

View toward the northeast from Campus Park with Rancho San Joaquin Golf Course in background, 1969.

in new UC President David Pierpont Gardner, who successfully lobbied Sacramento for greater support. Gardner found an unexpected ally in Governor George Deukmejian.

It was clear, however, that if UC Irvine was to grow as rapidly as its ambitions, the funds would have to come from private sources, not the state. The chancellor asked the university's loyal support groups to pick up the slack. The Friends of the University of California, Irvine had always seen themselves more as "friend-raisers" than "fundraisers," but that changed. Other groups enlisted for fundraising included Town and Gown, the Big I Boosters (for athletics) and the Chancellor's Club, the last consisting of donors who contributed $1,000 or more annually. Private donations, which had been a modest $700,000 in 1972, surpassed $10 million in 1983. Even that sum paled compared to the huge losses in state funding.

Yet another drain on finances had arrived in 1976, when UC Irvine inherited the Orange County Medical Center from the county. The hospital catered mostly to poor patients, and the cost was high. There was scant reimbursement for patients who could not pay, and rates could not be raised high enough on the small number of well-to-do patients to close the gap. UCI's medical faculty considered the old facilities inadequate for a teaching hospital, and under the tenacious leadership of Dean Stanley van den Noort, they began a determined push for an on-campus teaching hospital.

The issue came to a head in 1983. UCI's bid for a hospital faced competition from a community group wanting to build a new hospital. It became clear that only one hospital would be approved—and it wouldn't be the university's. Aldrich decided enough was enough. He withdrew the campus hospital proposal. As he said later: "We needed in the long haul the support of the community, and I wasn't about to let this become the element for alienating the university further from the community."

Medical and other faculty members were furious with Aldrich and voted to censure him. Aldrich announced he would resign after the 1983–1984 academic year. As his retirement approached, the campus bid a grateful farewell. The black-tie banquet required an enormous white tent to hold the 550 celebrants. After 22 years, then the longest tenure of any chancellor in UC history, the Aldrich era drew to a close.

October 16, 1974 Cross-Cultural Center founded in temporary building; moves to permanent building in 1989

June 1975 Men's tennis and men's golf win NCAA titles

September 1975 Children's Center opens by Verano Place

1976 The U.C. Eye *is first student-produced TV show*

January 1976 "The American Presidency" symposium includes Hubert Humphrey

February 1976 Matsue, Japan and Irvine Jaycees donate 50 cherry trees

July 1, 1976 Orange County Medical Center becomes UCI Medical Center

November 1976 Cross-country team wins second consecutive NCAA title

1979 Enrollment tops 10,000

November 15, 1979 Irvine Meadows West trailer park opens as affordable housing for students, faculty and staff

Jack W. Peltason

Chancellor 1984–1992

Jack W. Peltason often said: "The best affirmative action is expansion." Little wonder that he oversaw a period of rapid growth at UC Irvine. The student population grew by almost 50 percent—from fewer than 12,000 to almost 17,000. Private donations almost doubled from $10.2 million to $22.2 million. More than $500 million in new construction during his tenure included student and faculty housing, classrooms and labs.

A noted political scientist, he came to campus as a founding dean and vice chancellor, and soon presided over the academic plan. He left in 1967 to lead the University of Illinois at Urbana-Champaign, and then in 1977 took on the role of chief spokesman for higher education as president of the American Council on Education. He returned to UCI in 1984 to serve as chancellor. A gregarious leader who was not above donning goofy garb for UCI's Wayzgoose celebrations, Peltason created the UCI Medal, founded the Chief Executive Roundtable, and nurtured UCI's lucrative and still-thriving relationship with the business community.

"Jack Peltason's stewardship of UC Irvine … has been a national model of effective leadership," said William R. Schonfeld, dean of social sciences from 1982–2002. "He has always been a gentleman of great decency, wit, insight, wisdom, energy and commitment."

After he retired from UCI, the UC Regents tapped him for the presidency. During his three-year term, characterized by a bleak state budget, Peltason negotiated a multiyear funding compact with Governor Pete Wilson. In 2014, he was awarded the UC Presidential Medal for extraordinary service.

▼ *Chancellor Peltason leads the celebration in Aldrich Park for Wayzgoose, UCI's oldest student-run festival.*

▲ *Peltason with Peter the Anteater c. 1986.*

◄ *UC Irvine's second chancellor oversees a period of unprecedented growth in the campus's physical expansion, funding and enrollment.*

► *Commencement in the park, c. 1980.*

1980 UC Irvine wins Intercollegiate Sailing Association Sloop Championship (repeats win in 2005)

February 1980 Video game championship added to Engineering Week

December 4, 1980 Laser Microbeam Program (LAMP) laboratory opens

1981 UCI Libraries acquires one-millionth volume

March 1981 Basketball standout Kevin Magee named AP first-team All-American (he earns the same honor in 1982)

March 1982 F. Sherwood Rowland releases findings showing chlorofluorocarbons tripled over past decade

June 26, 1982 Alumnus Steve Scott breaks his own American mile record by running 3:48.53 (11 days later, he breaks it again, running 3:47.69, second-fastest in history)

September 1982 University Club opens after 10-year fundraising drive

December 1982 Professor Mark Baldassare releases first Orange County Annual Survey

1983 Women's cross-country team wins first of five consecutive PCAA titles

April 1983 English professor Charles Wright is corecipient of National Book Award for Poetry for Country Music: Selected Early Poems (his Black Zodiac wins Pulitzer Prize in 1998)

November 1983 Groundbreaking for Town Center; private donations rise 110 percent to $10,080,850

June 1984 500-plus people attend Aldrich's retirement dinner

June 6, 1984 Campus Park renamed to Aldrich Park

"UNDER CONSTRUCTION INDEFINITELY"

In October 1983, UC Irvine got a glimpse of its future. Ground was broken on the Nelson Research Center, a $6.5 million joint venture between the campus and Nelson Research & Development Co., an Irvine drug developer. The project introduced the novel idea that a large research building could be built on UCI land, even if it were privately financed and constructed. Joan Irvine Smith and her mother, Athalie Clarke, donated $2 million to speed the property transfer to the university.

Even as Aldrich was preparing to clean out his office, big things were happening at UC Irvine. Enrollment had topped 10,000 for the first time in fall 1979; by 1984, it had soared to 12,684. The campus embarked on a $400 million construction drive to make room for the burgeoning student population. Much of it was privately funded.

Jack Peltason, who returned to campus as its new chancellor in 1984 after leading the University of Illinois at Urbana-Champaign and the American Council on Education, had no less ambition than his predecessor—perhaps more. "I want Irvine to be mentioned in the same breath as Harvard and Berkeley," he unabashedly told the *Orange County Register*.

He found a bustling campus. Thousands of new students crammed the hallways, shielding their ears from the noise of a construction boom that was adding 40 new buildings. They were desperately needed to keep up with the influx of students, who gave UCI the tongue-in-cheek moniker of "Under Construction Indefinitely."

"The university was in an explosive growth," Peltason said in an oral history interview conducted by UC Berkeley. "We were coming into our own." He added: "One school year ... we had more buildings going up than we had in existence."

He made private fundraising a high priority. "There was the old cliché that the state will make us a good university, private dollars will make us a great university," he said.

Peltason and his chief fundraiser, John Miltner, met with Irvine Company Chairman Donald Bren shortly before Peltason's tenure began in October 1984. The main topic: money. Bren was eager to help, and he and the Irvine Company made some of the largest contributions to UC Irvine's growth. Peltason said later that Bren had "discovered that his visions for the university, UCI, were the same as mine." He said Bren "never asked me to do anything that was incompatible with my responsibilities. He's a very sophisticated person; he knows that donors cannot dictate terms and conditions. You can't buy a university; [he] always respected the integrity of it." Both Bren and inventor and entrepreneur Arnold Beckman gave millions of dollars for new buildings and facilities, including the Bren Events Center and the Beckman Laser Institute.

August 1984 Alumnus Greg Louganis wins two Olympic diving gold medals in Los Angeles (four years later, he earns two more in Seoul)

September 1984 Jack W. Peltason appointed chancellor

April 1985 Pedestrian bridge connecting UCI with University Town Center (named Watson Bridge in 2005) is dedicated

▼ *Chancellor Wilkening with Peter the Anteater, 1994.*

Laurel L. Wilkening

Chancellor 1993–1998

Before taking the reins as UC Irvine's third chancellor, Laurel Wilkening had served five years as provost at the University of Washington and had spent most of her career teasing secrets out of comets and meteorites. As a planetary scientist at the University of Arizona, she had served on numerous NASA committees and boards.

Her administrative experience and academic credentials left her uniquely prepared to turn her focus to attracting star faculty and critical private funding in an era of reduced state support. During her tenure, two UCI professors won Nobel Prizes (1995) and 250,000 square feet of construction was completed. Wilkening's goal to move UC Irvine into the ranks of America's top 50 research universities was realized in 1995. She was also instrumental in creating University Research Park—a complex of more than 100 businesses on campus whose CEOs can cross the street to interact with students and faculty. It created a national model for collaboration between the private sector and university researchers.

The Laurel L. Wilkening Rose Garden is testament to her calm, straightforward approach, which served the campus well as she battled a lingering recession. "She was very grounded, very centered," said Manuel Gomez, whom Wilkening appointed vice chancellor of student affairs. "She was a great leader for UC Irvine."

Wilkening retired to Arizona in 1998 to pursue projects that involved her personal passions of population growth, the global environment and women's issues.

▼ *The Laurel L. Wilkening Rose Garden, dedicated in 2005, features 365 rose bushes and serves as a reminder for the campus community to stop and smell the roses.*

▲ *Wilkening, UCI's third chancellor, and also the third female to serve as a campus chief executive in the University of California's first 125 years.*

◀ *The Bren Events Center on its opening in 1987.*

January 8, 1987 Bren Events Center opens with men's basketball claiming 118–96 victory over Utah State in front of a sellout crowd of 4,542

March 1987 Senior guard Scott Brooks named first-team All-PCAA for men's basketball; he led West Coast in scoring with 23.8 average

January 14, 1988 430-pound bronze statue of Peter the Anteater unveiled

April 16, 1988 West Coast headquarters of National Academies of Sciences and Engineering dedicated and named Arnold and Mabel Beckman Center after $20 million donation

February 1990 Students build "shantytown" protesting housing policies for gay couples

January 15, 1993 Laurel L. Wilkening appointed chancellor

1994 Engineering Gateway, Engineering Lecture Hall and Science Library open

April 12, 1994 Alumnus Yusef Komunyakaa receives Pulitzer Prize in poetry for Neon Vernacular, *and alumnus Michael Ramirez wins Pulitzer for editorial cartooning*

December 10, 1995 Nobel Prizes awarded to F. Sherwood Rowland (chemistry) and Frederick Reines (physics)

April 10, 1996 Alumnus Richard Ford receives Pulitzer Prize in fiction for Independence Day

April 16, 1998 Ralph J. Cicerone appointed chancellor

Peltason pushed relentlessly for endowments to hire and keep the best faculty, and for unrestricted funding they could use to do their work. How powerful was unrestricted funding? When F. Sherwood Rowland first found an "odd" sample of icy air from Antarctica, he needed to make sure it had not been contaminated. He used unrestricted funds to swiftly fly a graduate student back to Antarctica. He confirmed that the oddity was due to chlorofluorocarbon gas—a key discovery that eventually led to Rowland's Nobel Prize years later.

Peltason left UC Irvine in 1992 to fill the role of UC president, as Gardner retired. California had been hit by another recession, so severe that UC Irvine's enrollment dropped 2.5 percent that year. But Peltason used his political skills to negotiate a four-year deal with Governor Pete Wilson and the Legislature that temporarily stabilized the University of California, saving the system from what could have been a devastating multimillion-dollar loss.

Harsh realities greeted incoming Chancellor Laurel L. Wilkening in 1993. A planetary scientist and most recently provost at the University of Washington,

▲ *Pep squad, 1980–1981. First Row: L. Minaker. Second Row: T. Boyle, S. Coomber, M. Williams, L. Marino, T. Alexander. Third Row: R. Soward, T. Tabor, A. Ines.*

she grappled with plenty of bad news during her five-year tenure. Budget difficulties continued to drag on university finances. But news emerged in 1995 from Stockholm, Sweden, to brighten even the deepest gloom. UC Irvine became the first public university to have faculty win Nobel Prizes in two different fields—physics and chemistry, in this case—in the same year.

F. Sherwood Rowland, a founding faculty member in chemistry, had first theorized with graduate student Mario Molina in 1973 that chlorofluorocarbons were destroying the Earth's protective ozone layer. Despite withering attacks by chemical companies, Rowland conducted painstaking research that confirmed it. Within a few years, the American Chemical Society, the nation's largest professional society for chemists, lauded Rowland's discovery as one of the 10 most significant advances in chemistry of the 20th century. The other Nobel winner was Frederick Reines, a physics professor and founding faculty member who proved in 1956 with a colleague in South Carolina the existence of neutrinos, tiny subatomic particles released during nuclear reactions in stars.

When Wilkening retired in 1998, the *Los Angeles Times* noted that she had "won loyalty for pulling the university through in its darkest hour."

GLORY DAYS

Ralph J. Cicerone was one of Rowland's most accomplished colleagues in atmospheric research before he arrived at UC Irvine in 1989 to form the university's Earth system science department. After succeeding Wilkening as chancellor, he began building a new university hospital next to the old UCI Medical Center in Orange, and ramped up private fundraising. Cicerone understood that it was critical to replace state funding.

1999 Graduate School of Management ranked fifth in nation among "techno-MBA" programs by Computerworld

December 21, 1999 Henry Samueli School of Engineering named after $20 million gift

September 2000 UCI ranked 10th among public universities by U.S. News & World Report (in 2001 UCI tied for 10th with UC Davis and Georgia Institute of Technology)

December 7, 2000 Governor Gray Davis establishes California Institute for Telecommunications and Information Technology at UCI

April 16, 2001 Alumnus Michael Chabon receives Pulitzer Prize in fiction for The Amazing Adventures of Kavalier & Clay

December 1, 2002 UCI National Fuel Cell Research Center introduces highway-ready vehicle powered by hybrid electric fuel cell

▼ *Completed in 2003, John V. Croul Hall—named for philanthropist and cochair of Behr Processing Corporation—houses a three-story research center for the Department of Earth System Science.*

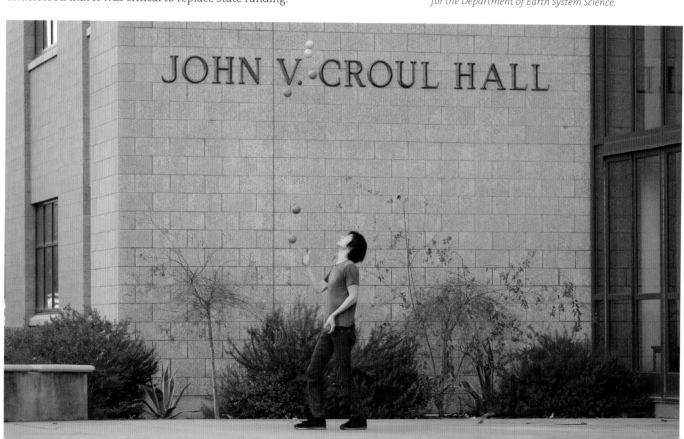

Ralph J. Cicerone

Chancellor 1998–2005

Ralph J. Cicerone arrived at UC Irvine in 1989 as an internationally acclaimed scientist in atmospheric chemistry, shortly thereafter founding the influential Department of Earth System Science. He served as dean of the School of Physical Sciences and then chancellor after Laurel L. Wilkening's retirement.

As a researcher, Cicerone had won the prestigious Bower Award for scientific achievement and was recognized on the citation for the Nobel Prize won by colleague F. Sherwood Rowland in 1995. He has frequently provided expert testimony to congressional committees.

"I learned a lot about the impact of research and how people do it at universities," Cicerone told UC Irvine historian and founding faculty member Spencer C. Olin. "But at the same time, I learned some practical things, like what are the rules of the federal agencies." He shared his expertise, advising younger faculty on how to apply for national grants.

Cicerone used his fundraising acumen to dramatically increase private giving to UCI. He recognized that a university must do more than great research—it must offer on-campus activities to attract the best students and donors. Cicerone helped revive UC Irvine's baseball program; Cicerone Field at Anteater Ballpark is named in his honor.

He oversaw construction of major research halls and the $375 million teaching hospital at UC Irvine Medical Center. And during his tenure, the campus notched its third Nobel Prize, won by Irwin Rose in chemistry.

Cicerone left UC Irvine in 2005 after being elected president of the National Academy of Sciences, where he wields international clout on scientific policymaking.

▼ *Inauguration of Cicerone, UCI's fourth chancellor, May 5, 1999.*

▲ *During Cicerone's seven-year tenure, UCI continues its climb in the national rankings and undergraduate admissions become more selective.*

◄ *Cicerone mingles with players on May 19, 2009, during the dedication of Cicerone Field, named after the driving force who helped reinstate baseball at UCI in 2002, and once played varsity himself at MIT.*

2004 Ted Newland retires as men's water polo coach with 714 victories, the most in NCAA history

December 10, 2004 Nobel Prize awarded to Irwin Rose (chemistry)

2005 English and creative writing professor Michael Ryan receives Kingsley Tufts Poetry Award for New and Selected Poems; Paul Merage School of Business named after $30 million gift

May 26, 2005 Michael V. Drake appointed chancellor

September 23, 2007 Regents approve Erwin Chemerinsky as School of Law's founding dean

March 2009 UCI's University Hospital (later renamed UC Irvine Douglas Hospital) opens on time and under budget

▼ *Sandblasting during construction of Social and Behavioral Sciences Gateway, dedicated in 2009.*

"To be a dean at UCI now ... it's virtually a requirement that the dean have a great deal of his or her emphasis on external activities to make our value known better to the community, so that they will be supportive politically and influentially, as well as through donations," he said in 2004. "We're finding an increasing number of people who understand the value of having a great university in their backyard. ... Is that going to solve the problem? I think it can."

Cicerone worked to get students and the community to spend more time on campus, particularly at night and on weekends. He urged campus officials to offer more performances and activities. He worked with Dan Guerrero, UCI's athletic director from 1992 to 2002, to bring back baseball as a Division I sport. "After a while, Irvine became more of a first-choice campus instead of a second-choice campus," Cicerone said. "We had more motivated students."

In 2004, there was more good news: a third Nobel Prize, won by Irwin Rose in chemistry. He shared the honor with two Israeli colleagues for research revealing the secrets behind spiral-shaped proteins that could be the culprits behind dozens of lethal diseases.

The increased activity also gave campus officials something to show potential donors. "Ambitious and generous individuals came on board," Cicerone said. "We had over $8 billion in construction the year after. We developed a record of getting things built right and maintained right."

Cicerone left UC Irvine in 2005 to lead the National Academy of Sciences. His successor, Michael V. Drake, who began his career as an ophthalmologist, made getting approval for a law school his first priority and succeeded where his predecessors had fallen short, stressing the benefit that a top law school could bring to Orange County and the region.

The bold choice of acclaimed scholar and activist Erwin Chemerinsky as dean brought the new school national attention. A guarantee of free tuition for the inaugural class attracted the best students, who outperformed those of many other respected law schools on their first bar exam. "We worked 24/7 to make all that happen," Drake said.

He set an ambitious goal for funding UC Irvine's continued growth and excellence: $1 billion over 10 years. By early 2014, the initiative was ahead of schedule, having collected more than $900 million. Drake emphasized the importance of "inclusive excellence," which tied together several themes that intertwine in UCI history: striving to make the campus one of the best in the world, caring for its students and encouraging diversity.

Michael V. Drake

Chancellor 2005–2014

Michael V. Drake put considerable energy into making sure a quality UC Irvine education remained accessible to a diverse student body, even as the university reluctantly raised fees in the face of state funding cuts. As a result, 40 percent of the Class of 2014 were first-generation college graduates.

He encouraged students, faculty and staff alike to pursue what he called the "four pillars of excellence": academic, research, leadership and character. "Ultimately, our goal is to educate the whole person," said Drake, an ophthalmologist and former vice president of health affairs for the University of California.

His vision of engaging law students as advocates in the community helped Drake persuade the UC Board of Regents to approve the UC Irvine School of Law. Opened in 2009, it garnered kudos when its first graduates bested every other California law school's graduates—except Stanford's—on the bar exam.

During Drake's tenure, students and faculty visited Ghana for cultural research and exchange; Israel and the Palestinian territories to enrich understanding of sociopolitical issues; and Kenya to build clean-water infrastructure. Under his leadership, the SAGE Scholars program connected low-income students with businesses for paid internships and scholarships. He embraced the Anteater community as his extended family, serving Thanksgiving dinner to more than 400 students who didn't go home for the holiday.

In one of his last efforts at affordability, Drake became the top individual fundraiser in the UC Promise for Education campaign, raising $21,000 by pledging to lead a community bike ride. An avid biker, he led 50 supporters on a tour of Irvine.

▲ *UCI's fifth chancellor, Michael V. Drake, greets chemistry grad student Jason Deckman during the 2008 Budget Write-In at Phineas Banning Alumni House.*

▼ *Drake, donning UCI gear for the New Student Convocation, with 2011 ASUCI student body president Vikram Nayuda on his left.*

Howard Gillman

Chancellor 2014–

Howard Gillman, appointed UC Irvine's sixth chancellor on September 18, 2014, entered college as a first-generation freshman at UCLA and quickly decided he would spend his life within the world of inquiry and discovery. He earned his doctorate there, became an award-winning scholar and teacher, and served as dean of the USC Dornsife College of Letters, Arts and Sciences before returning to the University of California in 2013 as UCI's provost and executive vice chancellor.

In nominating him for chancellor, UC president Janet Napolitano said: "Howard Gilman appreciates the entrepreneurial spirit and bold ambitions embodied by the campus, and he has the imagination, intelligence and energy to lead the faculty, staff and students to the next level of excellence."

Among his ambitious goals is ensuring that UCI attracts dynamic, diverse faculty committed to doing their very best work across all fields of inquiry, professional practice and creative expression. He is dedicated to providing a rich learning environment for students from all walks of life and looks for new ways to build on the campus's spirit of experimentation in academic experiences.

Gillman also nurtures UCI's special obligation in medicine, integrating leading academic clinicians and medical researchers into the community to more effectively fight disease and promote human health. There is hardly an area of study that does not contribute to this effort.

One of his first efforts as chancellor was establishing the Institute of Innovation. Its mission is to expand conversations and partnerships between the university and the region in order to move research into the marketplace more quickly.

As the vitally important anchoring institution for Orange County, Gillman believes the future of Orange County is inextricably linked to the ongoing development of UCI, and he works with regional leaders to advance shared goals and values.

▲ *Gillman, a first-generation college graduate and Southern California native is appointed UCI's sixth chancellor, September 18, 2014.*

▼ *Meeting members of the Spirit Squad during Welcome Week's Anteater Involvement Fair, 2014.*

◀ *UCI colors fly proudly next to the American flag near Anteater Plaza.*

May 5, 2012 First class graduates from School of Law

September 25, 2012 6,084 students break Guinness World Record for largest dodgeball game (in 2013, 3,875 UCI students set the Guinness World Record for largest water-gun fight and in 2014, 4,200 students set the record for the world's largest pillow fight)

May 4, 2013 Men's volleyball wins second consecutive NCAA title (its fourth in seven years)

June 19, 2013 UCI ranked fifth in world (first in nation) among universities under 50 years old by Times Higher Education *magazine*

June 14, 2014 President Barack Obama speaks at commencement at Angel Stadium of Anaheim

September 18, 2014 Howard Gillman appointed chancellor

As the campus closed in on its 50th anniversary, news came in 2014 that UC Irvine had been ranked seventh in the world and first in the nation among universities under 50 years old by *Times Higher Education* magazine.

Drake announced in early 2014 that he would leave UC Irvine to become president of The Ohio State University. Howard Gillman, provost and executive vice chancellor, was named interim chancellor and then chancellor in September 2014.

The university that had opened its doors to 1,589 students had more than 30,000 by fall 2014, and the faculty that initially numbered 119 exceeded 1,100. The eight original buildings students walked through have been joined by nearly 100 more. The campus, challenged by President Lyndon B. Johnson in his 1964 dedication speech to realize its dreams without limits, was acknowledged 50 years later by President Barack Obama in a commencement address as "ahead of the curve."

UC Irvine's early planners and leaders could hardly have imagined what the university would look like half a century later. Pereira's original vision for the campus has been altered significantly to adjust for changing times, as he understood it would. "I think he'd be amazed at some of the things we have done," Drake said shortly before his departure.

Added Gillman: "The fact that we are world-class but still relatively young is an incredible strategic advantage. We know what it means to operate at the highest levels, but we still have greater ambitions."

chapter 2

concrete inspiration

Distanced from Orange County's metropolitan core, a profound quiet must have enveloped the trio who in the early 1960s walked the rolling fields that would be home to the University of California, Irvine. Peering decades into the future, UC President Clark Kerr, Chancellor Daniel G. Aldrich Jr. and architect William Pereira surveyed the land's gentle ridges and small arroyos, blanketed with coastal sage and ancient seashells, as they discussed their vision for the campus.

▲ *Westward view of the campus, October 1966.*

◄ *Students on the veranda of the Humanities-Social Science Building (now Krieger Hall), April 1967.*

2

An Urban Forest and Phantom Campanile

The sprawling land selected by the University of California Board of Regents as home to the new university had few trees. Nevertheless, the original campus plans included the ambitious creation of a 21-acre "urban forest," filling the interior of Ring Mall. Commencements were held on a great lawn in Campus Park for many years. In 1984, the park was renamed Aldrich Park upon the founding chancellor's retirement, and graduation ceremonies were eventually moved to the Bren Events Center. Today, the park is a popular place for quiet study, napping, tossing Frisbees and occasional festivals, such as Celebrate UCI.

The park did not evolve entirely as envisioned. Architect William Pereira's plans called for construction of "the Centrum," a 250-foot-high, freestanding bell tower and museum situated in the park's center to give the campus an identifying architectural symbol. However, plans for the Brutalist, white, cast-concrete tower were sidelined by other priorities.

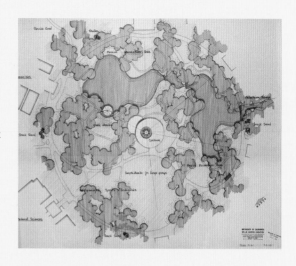

▲▲ *Original plans for the park include an intimate Greek theater and an "amphitheater for larger groups," as well as a towering campanile at its core.*

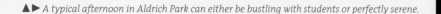

▲▶ *A typical afternoon in Aldrich Park can either be bustling with students or perfectly serene.*

Master planner William Pereira in 1966 with his ambitious plan for the campus, as he envisioned it in 1990

Inspiration came quickly—and was deceptively simple. During one of their early talks, Kerr drew a circle on a napkin to illustrate an idea: The campus would be built around concentric rings with six sectors, each representing an academic discipline. A central park would become the campus's metaphorical heart. Five academic units—biological sciences; humanities and fine arts; engineering and information and computer sciences; physical sciences and social sciences—and one administrative plaza with academic support facilities would cater to undergraduates. Specialized programs, research facilities and graduate education buildings would extend outward from the six sectors along radial spines, like the spokes of a wagon wheel.

The administrative plaza serving as the campus gateway would link to the adjacent commercial center, creating a true "town and gown" community. A circular, one-mile pedestrian corridor known as Ring Mall would provide easy access to campus buildings by foot or bike. Pereira cautioned against laying too many walkways through the park during the campus's initial construction. Better, he thought, to let the first students carve their own shortcuts. Once the grass on those paths had worn thin, the university would immortalize the routes with asphalt.

The ring design proved to be the university's defining physical characteristic. While one half was in place on opening day, future planners would complete the circle and adhere to the master plan, noted Wendell Brase, appointed vice chancellor of administrative and business services in 1991. "The master plan for this campus is as robust and effective as any I've ever seen," he said. "Many, many master plans for universities are abandoned after a few years. Using concentric circles and keeping cars on the outside were powerful ideas that prevailed over time."

Site preparation for the Commons and Library-Administration underway in late 1963.

Construction manager Earl Graham inspects central campus from temporary observation platform built for visitors, 1964.

37

▶ *In anticipation of the University of California's centennial in 1968, UC President Clark Kerr commissioned Ansel Adams to photograph the system's campuses, including the newly rising UC Irvine. Adams first visited campus in spring 1964, when "there was nothing at Irvine but a few skeletal piers." He encountered similar beginnings at UC San Diego and UC Santa Cruz. "The excitement of seeing so many plans, hope and ideas materializing simultaneously embraced not only the University, from Regents to freshmen, but also the surrounding communities," wrote Adams and photography critic Nancy Newhall. Adams returned several times to capture the campus as it developed, with his last visit in spring 1967. Many photographs from that visit grace the pages of this book. They were published in the commemorative book,* Fiat Lux: The University of California, *and reside in the California Museum of Photography, UC Riverside.*

IN LOVE WITH CONCRETE

The UC Board of Regents approved designs for the initial buildings in fall 1962, and construction began in early 1964. The first eight permanent buildings were: Campus Hall (now Crawford Hall), Central Plant, Science Lecture Hall (now Schneiderman Lecture Hall), Biological Sciences I, Library-Administration (now Langson Library), Humanities/Social Sciences (now Krieger Hall), Commons (now Gateway Study Center) and Humanities Hall.

Early Pereira-designed buildings earned both admirers and critics. Explaining that the buildings should guard their inhabitants from the glare of the California sun, Pereira used prefabricated, reinforced concrete panels to create boxy structures. While considered durable and strong, some of the structures were built on a pedestal-like ground floor so that the bulk of the building seems to almost float above pedestrians below. The style, called Brutalism, was popular among mid-20th century architects. Some praised the structures as starkly beautiful and futuristic, hinting at the technological era that was to come. Others called the style cold and impersonal.

Ansel Adams at Library-Administration, 1966.

▲ *Central campus construction, June 1965.*

"I'll never forget when one of the Planet of the Apes *movies was filmed on our campus. There were apes running all over, attending classes, socializing with students and generally attracting an enormous amount of attention!"*

—Beverly Bostwick Mulherin '76

◀ *Students mingle with cast and crew of* Conquest of the Planet of the Apes *during a filming break, 1972, with the Engineering Tower providing a Brutalist backdrop.*

Several other movies have had scenes shot on location at UCI over the years. They include:

Silent Movie *(1976)*
Poltergeist *(1982)*
Creator *(1985)*
Ocean's Eleven *(2001)*
The Hangover Part III *(2013)*

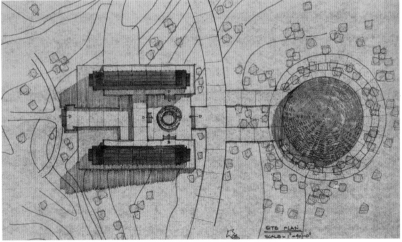

◀▲ *Site plan drawings depicting Pereira's architectural vision.*

▼ *Early signs of construction, July 1964.*

▼ ▶ *The beginnings of Library-Administration, and in its completed form, December 1966.*

"*There is something photographically magnetic about UCI which makes a photographer desire to have his camera with him at all times.*"

—**Stu Shaffer**
INAUGURAL YEARBOOK PHOTOGRAPHER

Towering Above All

Completed in 1970, the distinctive Engineering Tower is one of the campus's most iconic buildings:

- At nine stories, it's the tallest structure on campus and its rooftop is a favorite spot for watching Disneyland's fireworks
- The tower was originally built with only men's bathrooms because there were no female engineering students or faculty
- Once home to behemoth, room-sized computers that were installed by opening up entire walls, now the building contains sealed panels that mark where those computers were once hoisted into place
- A completely symmetrical building, students had trouble finding the entrance until a red archway was added to rescue those late for class

◀ *Workers remove precast concrete forms from the wall of Library-Administration as work to double the size of the building begins, June 1968.*

The fortress style reflects the era in which they were built, noted Rebekah Gladson, who was appointed campus architect in 1992. With antiwar and civil rights demonstrations raging nationwide, the buildings created a hard barrier to the outside world. The structures did not promote human interaction, but as Gladson said at a 2005 symposium celebrating the campus's 40th anniversary: "The Pereira buildings created strong visual objects around a pedestrian Ring Mall and started the delineation of a place. ... Brutalism as a style was often associated with social utopian ideology. What could be more socially optimistic than the creation of a new university?"

While other architects who contributed to the early campus also favored Brutalism, the emphasis during the first five years after the campus opened was on building quickly. Verano Place, apartment-style student housing, was finished in 1966 and the Medical Surge Buildings I and II in 1968 and 1969. The Physical Sciences Building, Fine Arts Village, Engineering Building and Student

▲ The campus, with Engineering Tower in the center, as seen from the San Joaquin Marsh Preserve, a UC Natural Reserve System, 1970s.

◄ A rare color campus aerial from summer 1968, showing a half-completed main campus.

42

Health Center were also completed by the end of 1971. That spurt marked the closing of the ring, and tight state budgets slowed the pace of construction funding in the 1970s.

IN SEARCH OF AN IDENTITY

In the 1980s, a $400 million construction boom resulted in almost 40 new facilities rising on campus and at the UC Irvine Medical Center in Orange. The land surrounding Ring Mall was largely built up, but other areas of campus, such as University Hills to the south and student housing in the east, began to fill in. UC Irvine leaders had turned to private support to spur development.

In April 1984, the Irvine Company donated $1 million toward the Bren Events Center, which would house the burgeoning basketball program and dozens of annual ceremonies and events central to student life. The Arnold and Mabel Beckman Foundation donated $2.5 million for the Beckman Laser Institute and Medical Clinic, an interdisciplinary center for the development and application of optical technologies in biology and medicine. Opened in 1986, it helped solidify the university's reputation in biotechnology. The 1990 debut of the 750-seat Irvine Barclay Theatre represented a joint project of the university, the city of Irvine and the private sector.

Ring Mall, the 21-acre Campus Park and Brutalist architecture gave UC Irvine a unique physical identity. But by the early 1980s, amid enormous

▲ *A key feature of Brutalist windows, including those of Rowland Hall, were intended to keep out the hot California sun.*

▼ *Humanities Bridge opens up onto a newly planted Campus Park, 1966.*

▼ *The Fine Arts Pedestrian Bridge spans West Peltason Drive, connecting humanities with the fine arts.*

> *"Many seniors may remember the old shortcut that was worn into the hill between Fine Arts and Humanities. It was dirty, but it was great. One morning, without warning, it was gone and we were face-to-face with an appalling Rent-A-Fence and the fact that we were going to be very late to class."*
>
> —A 1999 YEARBOOK EDITOR ON THE BUILDING OF THE FINE ARTS BRIDGE

physical expansion, campus planners and architects sought to free themselves from design constraints. "Campus leaders felt that the Pereira buildings were too much alike," Brase said. "The campus hired architect David Neuman, who really believed in putting Irvine on the map. Almost every building designed in the '80s won architectural prizes."

Diverse aesthetic styles and structures defined the postmodern phase of architecture: McGaugh Hall, built by Canadian architect Arthur Erikson and dubbed "the Emerald City" for its green hue; Charles Moore's Italian Renaissance-style University Extension and Alumni House; Robert Stern's Studio Four of the Claire Trevor School of the Arts; the Paul Merage School of Business "decorated shed" building, designed by Robert Venturi; and celebrated British architect James Stirling's Science Library with its central courtyard.

The result was a collage of buildings that elicited strong love or hate reactions. Chancellor Jack W. Peltason called the new phase of architecture "adventuresome" and refused to join the lively debate about the green hue of the newly completed McGaugh Hall. "I'm not paid to like the color," he said, according to historian Samuel Clyde McCulloch's *Instant University*.

▶ *While its graduate programs were strongly influenced by the work of French philosopher and literary critic Jacques Derrida, who taught for nearly 20 years in UC Irvine's School of the Humanities, the physical landscape during the campus's Postmodernist phase was also much influenced by the deconstructionist period of the 1980s. Designed by Frank Gehry, the controversial Information and Computer Science and Engineering Facility, completed in 1989, contains a classroom block and a research wing joined to faculty offices by a prominent galvanized, sheet metal-clad stair tower. More than a decade later, considered not a good use of space, the building was torn down (with Gehry's blessing) and in its place now stands Engineering Hall. Gehry also designed two other campus buildings: the Information Computer Science/ Engineering Research Facility (1986) and the Rockwell Engineering Center (1990).*

◀ *The noticeable green tint of McGaugh Hall, originally Biological Sciences II completed in 1991.*

▼ *Anteater colors are visible in the blue and gold tile adorning the 287,000 square foot UCI Student Center, dedicated in 2007.*

UNITED THEY STAND

The number of campus buildings increased from eight in 1965 to 87 by 1990. Whether the buildings of the 1980s and early '90s were viewed as idiosyncratic or inspirational, Gladson faced a particular challenge when she assumed the role of campus architect: Unite the disparate styles and create a sense of place.

Gladson espoused a design aesthetic called contextualist architecture. Future buildings, she said, would have a distinct bottom, middle and top; would be sensitive to their neighbors; and would convey a sense of permanence and quality. Gladson believed that architecture should reflect people's wants and needs. She worked closely with students in designing the spirited gold-brick and blue-tile Student Center, which opened in 2007. The Social & Behavioral Sciences Gateway building, completed in 2009, also featured colored brick. The Anteater Recreation Center, opened in 2000, was barnlike in shape as a reminder of the university's agrarian roots. New buildings were situated to create plazas between groups of structures. In 2009 "as soon as the humanities buildings were completed, it created a plaza," Brase recalled. "People from around the campus started calling me saying, 'We want a plaza that looks like that.'"

Recent attempts to create gathering spots reflect what university leaders and historians cite as perhaps the only flaw in the university's master plan: The Brutalist buildings sit on Ring Mall but don't open onto it, somewhat isolating the park. Future campus development will address adding life to the park, perhaps by placing a building among the trees to attract staff and students in need of conversation or a cup of coffee. Moreover, while some universities have run out of land to build upon, UCI's campus is not yet fully built out, Gladson said, and has the potential for 30 percent more square-footage growth.

"UCI has always believed in growth with excellence," Brase said. "We can expect our student population to expand and change, research priorities to evolve, and new technologies to be implemented, and our long-range plans can accommodate that kind of change. We are building for the future."

Going Green

Cool. Green. Sustainable. Those words characterize UC Irvine. The campus has ranked among *Sierra* magazine's top 10 "Coolest Schools" in recent years—and was first in 2014—for promoting Earth-friendly policies in life, work and education—and by involving students in that cause.

The campus boasts programs on waste diversion and recycling, water conservation, energy efficiency and reducing auto traffic. Its National Fuel Cell Research Center operates a station where drivers of hydrogen-powered cars can fill their tanks. UC Irvine's Smart Labs initiative reduces energy use in research labs, which accounts for as much as two-thirds of the campus's energy expenditures.

UCI has also collected 11 LEED Platinum ratings from the US Green Building Council. The Leadership in Energy and Environmental Design accreditations are based on sustainable design along with building and resource efficiency.

Sustainability extends to the landscaping too. The 1995 launch of the Green and Gold Plan led to the use of native, drought-tolerant plants. "Environmentalism is a value at UC Irvine," said Richard Demerjian, director of environmental planning and sustainability. "It goes back to the founding chancellor, who was a soils scientist. He was a champion of environmental issues."

▶ *The 72- x 49-foot Amonix solar panels on the ARC Sports Field rise 50½ feet high, and at peak power production generate 113 kilowatts that connect to the UCI microgrid and the Anteater Recreation Center.*

◀ *The first student residences completed on campus, Mesa Court, with its two- or three-story, apartment-like units, defied the traditional high-rise dormitories that were a staple of 1960s architecture.*

◀ *Engineering Gateway provides a route through Engineering Plaza and serves as a heavily used entry point for walkers coming to campus from University Hills.*

▲ *A study group makes perfect use of Aldrich Park on a typical Southern California sunny day, March 2014.*

▼ *Original lampposts, such as this one in 1967 under the Humanities Bridge, remain throughout campus today.*

▶ *The 19-acre Aldrich Park provides plenty of space for respite or myriad activity.*

◀ *Infinity Fountain, with its resident ducks, Harold and Maude, is a popular campus gathering spot. Getting a photograph taken while wading in its waters is a must on many students' pre-graduation to-do lists.*

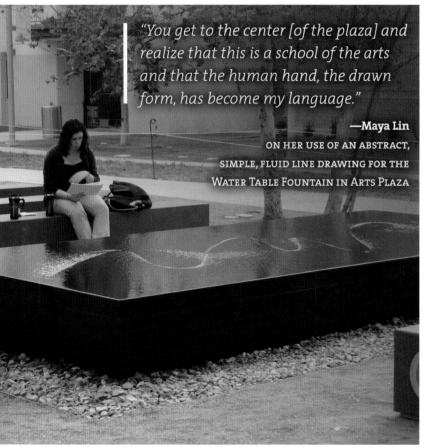

"You get to the center [of the plaza] and realize that this is a school of the arts and that the human hand, the drawn form, has become my language."

—Maya Lin

ON HER USE OF AN ABSTRACT, SIMPLE, FLUID LINE DRAWING FOR THE WATER TABLE FOUNTAIN IN ARTS PLAZA

The eight-story Social Sciences Tower, completed in 1971, is part of the social sciences complex designed by Albert C. Martin.

▲ *Architect Arthur Erickson's McGaugh Hall keeps the faith of Pereira's futurist technological optimism. Many biology students liken the building's abstract, robotic-looking design to a plant cell.*

▲ *The Medical Education Building in UCI's School of Medicine receives the top certification for sustainable construction— LEED Platinum—from the US Green Building Council in 2012.*

◀ Views of the Brutalist-inspired Science Lecture Hall (renamed Howard Schneiderman Lecture Hall in 2003 after the second dean of the School of Biological Sciences) amid still unmanicured landscaping, April 1967.

▼ Pereria's master plan of Brutalist buildings, including Rowland Hall designed by Kenneth S. Wing, explore the sculptural potential of concrete, utilizing technological advances of the time that add to their structural strength and durability.

► *Construction manager surveys the view in 1965 from Humanities-Social Sciences (renamed Krieger Hall in 2000).*

▲ *The year-old campus takes shape, 1966.*

◄ *Porch of Science Lecture Hall as captured by the lens of Ansel Adams, January 1966.*

► *Students traverse the road bordering Campus Park, December 1966.*

"Often referred to as 'the celebration of concrete' ... brutalism as a style was often associated with social utopian ideology. What could be more socially optimistic than the creation of a new university?"

—Rebekah Gladson
ASSOCIATE VICE CHANCELLOR AND
CAMPUS ARCHITECT SINCE 1992

▼ *Pereira at the Science Lecture Hall, December 1966.*

▶ *Student pauses on the steps of a newly opened building, December 1966.*

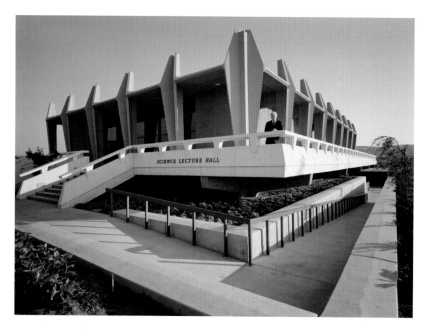

▲ Newly planted landscaping in spring 1966, and
▶ almost five decades later in 2014. There are more
than 11,000 trees and shrubs in Aldrich Park.

▼ Landscape architect Gene Uematsu, 1963.

► *The view north toward the physical sciences with Jamboree Road skyline in background.*

▼ *The glass-encased stairway of Engineering Hall.*

◄ *Frederick Reines Hall, named for the Nobel laureate, is characteristic of Postmodern architecture.*

"The acronym 'UCI' has been given an alternate meaning ever since [the Irvine Company provided 1,000 acres of land]. It is often said that the campus has been "under construction indefinitely."

—Rachel Sandoval

UCI HISTORICAL RECORDS PROJECT ARCHIVIST, 2005

A bird's eye view southward over the Claire Trevor School of the Arts (foreground) and central campus, 2002.

chapter 3

bucking academic tradition

In 1962, Daniel G. Aldrich Jr. and his wife, Jean, stopped in Honolulu en route home from Japan where Aldrich, a soils scientist, had taught California-style agriculture to farmers. Aldrich had just been appointed chancellor of the new University of California campus at Irvine. He was scheduled to present a tentative academic plan to the UC Board of Regents. In his room overlooking Waikiki Beach, he jotted down some ideas. The notes—which he kept in his personal records for decades— described a vibrant university "in the land-grant tradition of teaching, research and service" but tailored to an urban society.

▲ *The first academic convocation, in Aldrich Park, finds students surrounded by vast undeveloped horizons and a towering Engineering Hall.*

◄ *Raw campus environment is a clean slate for students and faculty on first day of classes, October 4, 1965. Buildings are Fine Arts, left, and Humanities-Social Sciences (now Krieger Hall).*

◀ *Howard Lawson, Friends of UCI Library and B.N. Desenberg, president of UCI Library, at a reception hosted by the Aldriches at University House, May 20, 1965.*

▲ *Samuel Clyde McCulloch, dean of humanities, and James G. March, dean of social sciences, talk to a prospective student, 1965.*

Aldrich had taken great care with the selection of the inaugural 119 faculty members. He recruited Ivan Hinderaker, who chaired political science at UCLA, to spearhead faculty hiring. Hinderaker quickly keyed in on two recruits: Edward A. Steinhaus, a UC Berkeley professor of pathobiology whom he tapped for dean of biological sciences, and Jack W. Peltason, who had served as dean of the College of Liberal Arts and Sciences at the University of Illinois before assuming the same role at UC Irvine.

Through cajoling, networking or sheer fortuitousness, other impressive appointments followed. Ralph W. Gerard was hired as dean of the Graduate Division and succeeded in establishing graduate programs in time for opening day in 1965. Samuel Clyde McCulloch, who later took on the role of official university historian, was appointed dean of humanities. Known for his emphasis on critical thinking, James G. March was hired as dean of social sciences, while Clayton Garrison accepted the position of dean of fine arts, vowing to create a vibrant school based on a conservatory approach. Frederick Reines, who was already internationally recognized for his discovery of the free neutrino while at Los Alamos National Laboratory, took on the position of dean of physical sciences. Bernard Gelbaum came aboard to chair mathematics, while F. Sherwood Rowland was hired to chair chemistry. James L. McGaugh was named chair of psychobiology and Hazard S. Adams chair of English.

◀ *From left, Edward A. Steinhaus, dean of the School of Biological Sciences, McCulloch and Hazard S. Adams, English department chair, at commencement 1967.*

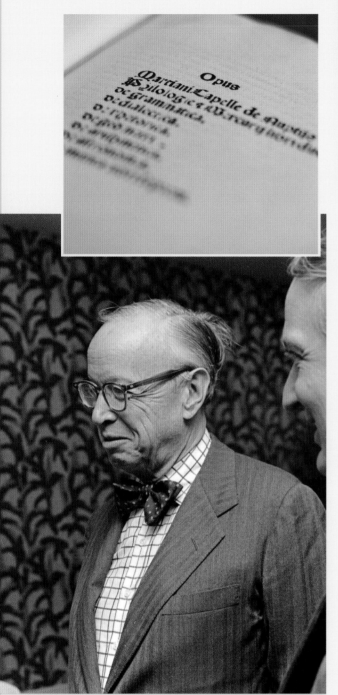

▲ *Early years are all about books and paper—not a computer in sight.*

◀ *McCulloch (left) with historian and keynote speaker Arthur Schlesinger Jr. in 1981 celebrating the library's millionth acquisition, Martianus Capella's* De Nuptiis Philologiae et Mercurii *(The Marriage of Philology and Mercury), 1499.*

Bookish from the Start

UC Irvine founders placed a priority on opening the university with a notable library. The debut collection of 100,000 books was 10,000 more than projected, owing to the resourcefulness of the first librarian, John E. Smith. In 1964, Smith wrote to faculty members asking for a list of 100 to 150 books they would expect to find in a university library.

UC President Clark Kerr helped too. UC San Diego was already under construction, and Kerr asked colleagues there to buy two extra copies of each book they purchased for their own campus: one copy for Irvine and one for the new campus in Santa Cruz.

UC Irvine's library grew rapidly, acquiring its millionth volume in 1981 and earning a ranking among the 100 top research libraries in North America. Historian Arthur Schlesinger Jr. spoke to an overflow crowd at the millionth-volume celebration.

The campus now supports four distinct libraries containing more than 3 million books and several hundred thousand journals, documents and audio-visual materials. Special Collections preserves 581 archival collections comprising more than 1 million original documents and photographs, including a rare copy of Shakespeare's First Folio. The edition was a gift from UC Irvine alumnus Patrick J. Hanratty, known as the father of computer-assisted design and manufacturing. The one-of-a-kind Southeast Asian Archive documents the struggles and triumphs of immigrants from Cambodia, Laos and Vietnam through everything from paintings by artists in refugee camps to business directories for Orange County's Little Saigon.

> *"A university's library plays a central role in recruiting and supporting the work of students and faculty alike."*
>
> —Christine Dormaier '70
> PRESIDENT, UCI CHANCELLOR'S CLUB, 2005

▲ Evolving fashion trends facilitate sitting cross-legged among the stacks at Langson Library.

► Library-Administration, December 1966.

►► Students Kelvin Lee (left) and Kevin Tanaka Jr. (right) and alumna Natasha Zubair compare notes outside Langson Library.

"The 100,000-volume opening day collection was larger than any academic library heretofore in this nation."

—Calvin J. Boyer
UNIVERSITY LIBRARIAN, 1980–1991

▲ *Rifling through periodicals is a common research strategy before computers.*

◀ *Study session with smart phone and other electronic aids at the ready.*

The inaugural faculty shaped the curricula and values underlying the pursuit of knowledge at UC Irvine: a commitment to excellence, a pioneering spirit and a willingness to apply novel approaches to education. They possessed the self-reliance needed to succeed as an upstart along with the flexibility conducive to rapid change. "They were people of vision," said Professor William H. Parker, who joined the faculty in 1967.

Moving to UC Irvine "was an irresistible challenge—in effect, a clean slate backed by the power of the state of California and by the well-earned educational reputations of the sister campuses of the university," recalled Rowland in a 1999 student yearbook interview. "I was then 36 years old—Chancellor Aldrich was in his early 40s—and most of our colleague chairmen were in the same age range. As we gathered in what is now North Campus looking across at the first permanent buildings under construction, change was underway, but the future looked exciting and promising while full of unknowns."

Sometimes their unbridled enthusiasm for the future was unnerving. Gerard, an authority on the brain, pushed hard for a computer-based campus. McCulloch recalled, "He shook up librarian John E. Smith when he said: 'The traditional library [is] as dead as the dodo.'" Reines, meanwhile, was attracted to the blank-slate campus. "I wanted to go to a new venture, someplace that was growing, ever growing, ever changing," he said in 1990. He was also impressed with Aldrich's enthusiastic support of his faculty, a sentiment widely shared by others.

In a 1990 interview, William J. Lillyman, who joined UCI in the early 1970s, said: "I think Dan [Aldrich] never felt that he had to do everything himself, that he was giving others opportunity to develop themselves, and he was genuinely pleased when he saw people doing good things. And he was right, because an institution like UCI takes a lot of good people doing a lot of good things to make it happen."

The founding faculty took interest in one another's projects and understood that success for one benefited all. "I always felt the faculty that was here in the beginning had a special bond,"

▲ *F. Sherwood Rowland, fourth from left, and chemistry department faculty members inspect Natural Sciences Building, now Steinhaus Hall.*

▼ *From left, Samuel Clyde McCulloch, dean of humanities; Jack W. Peltason, vice chancellor, academic affairs; and Florence Arnold, administrative assistant, begin the move from interim offices to central campus, August 1965.*

◄ *Diane O'Dowd, vice provost for academic personnel and professor of developmental and cell biology, advocates for creative excellence in teaching.*

Peltason in 2004 told Spencer C. Olin, an original faculty member and dean of humanities from 1992–1996. "Friendships were made and solidified much faster in those first years because we were all pioneers, all new."

Many of the early recruits remained on campus for decades, committed to ensuring its success. "One of the most critical decisions the founders made 50 years ago was to hire a tremendous collection of faculty who not only set the stage but continued to drive the university forward," said Howard Gillman, appointed provost and executive vice chancellor in June 2013 and chancellor in September 2014. "It underscores how fundamentally important it is to get a strong faculty who are eager to address the most important issues facing the world and want to build exciting, globally preeminent programs.

▼ *Maria Pantelia with print and digital versions of Thesaurus Linguae Graecae.*

Ode to Greek Literature

UC Irvine's Thesaurus Linguae Graecae is the world's first database of Greek literature from antiquity to the present. Established in 1972 with a $1 million gift from alumna Marianne McDonald, a former UC Irvine doctoral student who now is a professor of theater and classics at UC San Diego, it has been generously supported by the David and Lucille Packard Foundation and the National Endowment for the Humanities, among others.

The ancient Greeks wrote extensively about the debut of Western civilization, but few texts remain. Thesaurus Linguae Graecae seeks to collect the entire corpus of surviving Greek literature for preservation and scholarly pursuit. The collection currently includes more than 105 million words of Greek text from Homer and beyond in 12,000 volumes and is available online to researchers.

"Students and scholars worldwide are studying Greek authors such as Homer and Plato in ways that were unimaginable a few decades ago."

—**Maria Pantelia**
DIRECTOR, THESAURUS LINGUAE GRAECAE

▼ *Ready for the 1967 commencement processional, from left, McCulloch, Peltason and Donald Walker, vice chancellor student affairs.*

▼ *Assistant professor Marjorie C. Caserio is the second chemist hired. Her stint as chair of the Academic Senate coincides with controversy over whether to situate the Nixon Library at UCI.*

Some of the folks were already incredibly accomplished but did their best work after they got here."

BREAKING THE MOLD

During his dedication address on June 20, 1964, Vice Chancellor Peltason was forced to improvise, as President Lyndon B. Johnson's helicopter was late. Peltason began to elaborate on the academic organization and instructional methodology soon to be known as the Irvine Plan. Five divisions—biological sciences, fine arts, humanities, physical sciences and social sciences—would form the basic units. But no school would be insulated. The plan required students to enroll in courses outside their major and complete classes in the hard sciences. Graduate degree programs were to be measured in terms of knowledge and competencies rather than hours spent in class. The first plan was printed in a booklet called the "purple book" for the color of its cover.

Finding where to go to class is a challenge on opening day, October 4, 1965.

◀ *Founding faculty members James L. McGaugh, right and Norman Weinberger, professors of neurobiology and behavior, reminisce.*

Considered a trailblazing philosophy in the 1960s, the Irvine Plan doubled as a major faculty recruiting tool.

From the outset, UC Irvine bucked academic tradition. The first academic plan, issued in 1963, called for a college of arts, letters and sciences, with Peltason as inaugural dean. But when Hinderaker left UC Irvine to become chancellor at UC Riverside in 1964 and Peltason assumed his job, the five divisional deans in the college saw an opportunity to further overthrow convention. They asked Aldrich to scrap plans for a dean and designate their divisions as separate schools. UC President Clark Kerr supported the idea.

McGaugh, in 1989, described the event as an early turning point. "What that did was to give us a 'school' structure rather than a liberal arts structure, and we are a different institution as a consequence of that," McGaugh said. "That almost-accidental occurrence has as much to do with the shape of us as anything else that ever happened."

LET FREEDOM RING

The decision to break up the college unleashed a spirit of innovation. Julian Feldman, an original faculty member in social sciences, joked in a 1990 interview that in those early days, "if somebody raised their hand, a new department was established." Deans and division chairs seized the opportunity to avoid the bureaucracy they had experienced at former institutions.

Edward Steinhaus forged ahead with a program he called the "new biology"—an innovation that established UC Irvine's reputation for innovation in the biological sciences. He dispensed with traditional departments, such as botany and physiology, and created interdisciplinary units at the forefront of the field, such as molecular biology. The resulting "UCI model" for biological sciences was copied nationally. Steinhaus also assigned the psychobiology department to biological sciences, acting on his prescient view of psychology as a brain-based science. He recruited McGaugh as psychobiology chairman, and in 1964, McGaugh received a US Public Health Service grant for cutting-edge research on brain functions in learning and memory.

"It was Ed who had the brilliant idea, I think, that psychobiology ought to be developed within biological sciences because, as he put it, it was too important to be left for the psychologists alone," McGaugh said in 1989. "Who could ask for anything more exciting, interesting, rewarding? ... It was just an incredible experience."

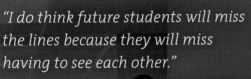

"I do think future students will miss the lines because they will miss having to see each other."

—**Jack W. Peltason**

CHANCELLOR 1984–1992, WRYLY WARNED IN 1988 AS COMPUTERIZED REGISTRATION WAS ON THE HORIZON

▼ *Biological sciences students take advantage of UCI's proximity to Newport Harbor.*

◀ *Campus community celebrates the naming of Francisco J. Ayala School of Biological Sciences, March 12, 2014. Front row from left, Gregory Leet, vice chancellor university advancement; Howard Gillman, provost and executive vice chancellor (later named chancellor); Francisco Ayala, University and Bren Professor of Ecology and Evolutionary Biology; Hana Ayala; and Frank LaFerla, Ayala school dean.*

▼ *Designed by James Stirling, the Francisco J. Ayala Science Library is the last Postmodern building erected on campus. Stirling's design creates an impressive stand-alone structure that pushes the very limits of its boundaries.*

The school's reputation was further advanced by the 1969 appointment of Howard Schneiderman, a brilliant scientist who soon took the helm as dean of biological sciences. He insisted that every biology student take humanities classes to improve writing skills. Biological sciences grew into one of the most popular majors, and UCI is now ranked among the top 20 colleges in the nation in developmental and cell biology.

Pioneering work in the School of Social Sciences also contributed to a longstanding teaching philosophy that spread across campus. March emphasized interdisciplinary study, describing academic departments as "the enemies of intellectual life." He encouraged instructional innovations, such as computer learning. "The School of Social Sciences was an extraordinarily attractive environment for, amongst other reasons, there were no boundaries at all," William Schonfeld, a political science professor who joined the school in 1970, said in 1990. "No matter what you were trained in, you were invited to pursue the intellectual interests and the teaching interests [that] you had."

TO DO IS TO LEARN

The university introduced new instructional methods and robust laboratory and fieldwork early on, particularly in the schools of fine arts and, later, in social ecology. Garrison's conservancy-style approach to art, drama, music and dance enabled performance-centered activities and cohesion.

> *"There were a few women among the founders of UCI's faculty and they inspired and helped cultivate a culture of inclusiveness and diversity that provided an example of the success that women in science achieve."*
>
> —Susan V. Bryant
> PROFESSOR OF DEVELOPMENTAL AND CELL BIOLOGY SINCE 1969; DEAN OF THE SCHOOL OF BIOLOGICAL SCIENCES 2000–2006, VICE CHANCELLOR FOR RESEARCH 2006–2010

◄ *UCI's status as a power in dance starts with the program's founding chair, Eugene Loring, who also helped attract the legendary Donald McKayle to campus.*

▶ *Robert Cohen, founding drama department chair, says he knew within the first few weeks that he was at UCI to stay.*

He succeeded in part by recruiting faculty with lofty qualifications as professional performers and artists as well as academicians.

The faculty included John Coplans, director of the art gallery; Eugene Loring, chairman of dance; Mehli Mehta, conductor of the University Orchestra; H. Colin Slim, chairman of music; Robert Cohen, drama department chair; and Roger Wagner, conductor of the University Chorus. Over the years, the school has attracted such notable names as David Hockney in art and Donald McKayle in dance. "The school was founded with only five full-time faculty but with a large group of professionals who came at different times to teach and train," Garrison recalled. "It was a rich learning experience. People worked long hours, overextended themselves and took great delight in it."

The first fine arts program occupied eight rooms on the fourth floor of what is now Krieger Hall, said Cohen in an essay he wrote for the 2005 yearbook. "But we had a ferocious spirit! Our founding dean, Clayton Garrison, convinced us that we would quickly become one of the nation's premier arts schools and, fired with his

◄ *David Hockney, with his trademark shock of white hair, mingles with UCI artists and John Coplans, of the University Art Gallery, at a faculty art exhibit.*

▼ *Poster for the show is by John Van Hamersveld, known for his iconic art for Bruce Brown's film* Endless Summer.

▲ *Clayton Garrison (at right), dean of fine arts, and Maurice Allard, assistant professor of music, rehearse with students for performances of* The Marriage of Figaro.

▲ *Student in pop art studio, December 1966.*

▲ *Students, under the direction of Robert Cohen, rehearse* Oedipus Tyrannos *at Founders' Rock in Campus Park, December 1966.*

▶ Swan Lake *performance highlights UCI's influence in the dance world.*

▶▶ *Preparations backstage for* Swan Lake.

passion, we convinced our students." The school is now called the Claire Trevor School of the Arts in recognition of the late Academy Award-winning actress.

The families of Claire Trevor and her stepson, Donald Bren, donated $10 million to the school, which includes the Contemporary Arts Center and its state-of-the-art studios, lab spaces, and theater and design facilities. The Claire Trevor School of the Arts also maintains a satellite program in New York City where students can spend five weeks taking classes and attending performances. Campuswide, students are encouraged to participate in laboratory research, fieldwork, service projects and study-abroad programs.

UC Irvine's Undergraduate Research Opportunities Program helps students in any discipline find faculty mentors on campus as well as off-campus programs with industrial partners, national labs or other universities. The program, which publishes the annual *UCI Undergraduate Research Journal*, is considered one of the finest models for undergraduate research in the country.

Innovative online learning initiatives have also attracted national recognition. Social ecology professor Daniel Stokols' environmental psychology class launched on iTunes U in June 2012 as the school's first free online course. More than 214,000 people participated in its first year. Open Chemistry,

▲ *Keith Bangs consults on set design in the Production Studio, Claire Trevor School of the Arts.*

▲ *Myrona DeLaney, drama lecturer, in Smith Hall working on the Musical Theatre Revue, 2014.*

▼ *Men in Black singers deliver choral harmony.*

▲ *More than 66,000 students sign up for an online, no-credit course based on AMC's* The Walking Dead, *taught by UCI faculty. From left, Zuzana Bic, public health; Joanne Christopherson, social sciences; Sarah Eichhorn, mathematics; and Michael Dennin, physics and astronomy.*

the most comprehensive free chemistry series ever offered online when it made its debut in March 2013, was a joint project between UC Irvine Extension and chemistry professor James Nowick. Later that year, the university took on the largest experiment in "edutainment" to date and partnered with AMC and Instructure to produce online courses linked to the hit TV show *The Walking Dead*. Classes in public health, social sciences, physics and math tapped into popular culture while provoking rigorous, scientific discourse on the show's content.

TEACHING, RESEARCH AND PUBLIC SERVICE

Few programs typify UC Irvine's dedication to multidisciplinary study and experiential learning more than social ecology. Developed in 1970, it applies scientific methods to recurring social and environmental problems such as urban development, traffic engineering, city and county planning, and environmental planning. When the regents approved social ecology

▶ *Arnold Binder (right) makes the case for a School of Social Ecology.*

as a school in 1992, UC Irvine became the first US university to offer an undergraduate major in the field. Arnold Binder, who joined the psychology faculty in 1966, approached Aldrich with his idea of an interdisciplinary unit that would balance teaching, research and public service. Breaking the mold of traditional academic disciplines appealed to Aldrich.

"As Arnie unfolded this idea about social ecology, it struck me that this is essentially what I came here to Irvine to do," Aldrich said in the book *UCI: The First 25 Years,* by Suzanne Toll Peltason. William Parker said the program fit Aldrich's version of a land-grant college. "Dan saw Irvine addressing those modern issues the way the land-grant college of the 1850s and 1860s addressed the issues of the mid-19th century," he said. "Social ecology is an academic program that I think best exemplifies Dan Aldrich's vision."

Aldrich's "mission-oriented" approach remains intact. Social ecology students must complete 100 hours of field study before graduation. Each year, they contribute at least 75,000 community service hours in areas ranging from corrections and law enforcement to teaching and mentoring.

CROSSING DISCIPLINES BEFORE IT WAS POPULAR

A magazine interview with Aldrich in October 1965 focused on the university's trailblazing ambitions. "The professor who wants to grow old gracefully in ivy-covered buildings would not be at ease on this campus," Aldrich said.

Multidisciplinary scholarship, a key component of that vision, has been a driving force at UC Irvine since its inception, Chancellor Gillman said. "It's almost boilerplate language at every great institution today," he said. "But this faculty figured it out a long time ago. They demonstrated high aspirations and the intent that this institution was not going to copy its way to the top. That's important, because you can never copy your way to the top." Gillman added: "That combination of great ambition and willingness to think in new ways, given the youth of the place, serves this institution very well."

Another audacious decision that yielded remarkable results was the program in computer studies. Gerard established an initial course in computer science in the 1965–1966 academic year—despite a ferocious winter storm that flooded the computer lab. By 1967, students could major in information and computer science, and three years later, a computer science building opened. By the university's 10th anniversary, about 40 percent of students campuswide used computers in at least one class. Faculty saw them as tools to improve students' problem-solving skills.

Between 1998 and 2003, enrollment grew 125 percent as students flocked to the information and computer science program to study software engineering, computer architecture, artificial intelligence and the social aspects of computing, and 31 new faculty positions were created.

▲ *UCI, the first to establish an independent school of computer sciences, is also the first in the UC system to offer a major in computer game science.*

▼ *Fred Tonge Jr., founding faculty member in the Graduate School of Administration, and James March, social sciences dean, confer in the early computer facility.*

PUTER SCIENCE

In 2002, the program matured into the University of California's first computer science school. It was renamed the Donald Bren School of Information and Computer Sciences in 2004 in recognition of Bren's $20 million gift. It remains the only independent computer technology school in the UC system and excels in building liaisons with other academic disciplines such as biology, the arts, transportation and sociology. The multidisciplinary focus meets the growing demand for computer skills in the performing arts, bioinformatics and computational physics. Among its many nationally ranked programs, it has the distinction of being one of the few schools to offer a major in computer game science. The popular major saw its first graduates in 2014.

FORWARD THINKING

The university's noteworthy critical theory in literature programs also developed from unquenchable intellectual curiosity with the hiring of Murray Krieger. A leading scholar in literary criticism, Krieger sought to confront

▲ *Have laptop will travel.*
◄ *Students carry computers to communal study areas.*

▼ *Deconstructionist Jacques Derrida, center, now has his papers in UCI Libraries' Special Collections.*

the social, historical and ideological forces and structures that produce and constrain literature.

English chairman Hazard S. Adams and Krieger believed that literary theory should be central to the development of English departments. "We felt there ought to be some place in which English departments would consider some of the generic questions about the nature of literature and its creation and reception," Krieger said in 1990. Named a University Professor—the University of California's highest professorial rank—Krieger brought international recognition to UCI and recruited renowned permanent and visiting faculty, such as Etienne Balibar, Jacques Derrida, Wolfgang Iser, Jean-Francois Lyotard, J. Hillis Miller and Gayatri Chakravorty Spivak.

The only university in the country offering a doctorate in critical theory, UC Irvine was selected as founding campus for the National School for Criticism and Theory. While an undergraduate emphasis in comparative literature and critical theory is still offered, the critical theory emphasis for graduate students was expanded beyond literature to include other disciplines in the humanities. Scholars explore and develop theoretical models to analyze and critique cultural forms in literature, art, information systems,

Where Writers Find Their Voice

Few programs boast more illustrious alumni than the MFA Programs in Writing, housed in UCI's Department of English. The workshops in poetry and fiction enroll a select number of students to ensure close consultation with faculty.

Alumni include novelists Michael Chabon, Richard Ford, Alice Sebold, Jay Gummerman, Marti Leimbach and Whitney Otto, as well as poets Yusef Komunyakaa, Allison Benis White and Colette LaBouff Atkinson. Esteemed faculty include novelists Ron Carlson and Michelle Latiolais, as well as poet Michael Ryan, and nonfiction writers Rajagopalan Radhakrishnan and Amy Wilentz.

"I'd finish workshop and sometimes walk around Aldrich Park with a friend and intently discuss every word that had been said as we learned the editorial process of what to take and what to leave behind. ... UCI was my launching pad, with super-spring in its pad materials."

—Aimee Bender MFA '77
AUTHOR

▲ *UCI Drama Theatre Guild presents* The Trial of Dedan Kimathi *by UCI's renowned Ngũgĩ wa Thiong'o and Micere Githae Mugo, March 2014.*

▶ *There is no shortage of peaceful study spots in Aldrich Park.*

▲ *Krieger Hall stands as a monument to early influence by literary critic and theorist Murray Krieger.*

history, language, social and political relations, and issues of gender and ethnicity.

"Irvine had a head start on everybody else because Hazard and I were doing theory here before any other place was," Krieger said in 1990. "And so, as theory became more important, Irvine's position became more visible. ... I remember thinking perhaps how foolish it was and how idealistic—utopian perhaps—to think you could come to a new university and really create a distinguished place in a short amount of time. But now it is commonly said everywhere that for graduate students in literature, Irvine is one of the places they automatically think of."

The success of the critical theory program gave the university gravitas despite its newness. "UCI staked out a name for itself early on with this program," said Michael Clark, interim provost and executive vice chancellor. "The critical theory program has become internationally famous. J. Hillis Miller, Jacques Derrida and Jean-François Lyotard are internationally prominent people who will still be talked about decades from now."

THE MODERN LAND-GRANT UNIVERSITY

By its 25th anniversary, UC Irvine had joined the list of the nation's top 100 research institutions, and those studies were having an impact—even changing the world.

Academic inquiry that informs the public and improves quality of life is exactly what the university's founders had in mind. In the 1965 NBC documentary *Birth of a Campus*, Aldrich envisioned faculty and students engaged in national and international dialogue on issues of great public significance.

"Since Irvine sits in the middle of the most rapidly growing urban area in the country, with all of the problems attendant to the spread of people across a landscape, we're hopeful that out of our various disciplines will flow information that will assist people with solving the many problems that confront them," Aldrich said.

▶ *A classroom in the Paul Merage School of Business.*

Many of the university's research organizations are aimed at developing solutions to real problems. The national debate over immigration, so critical to California, is the focus of the Center for Research on Immigration, Population and Public Policy, established by the Academic Senate in 2001. The Center for Digital Transformation at The Paul Merage School of Business reflects the growing importance of digital technologies in business and society while the Institute of Transportation Studies grew out of the rapid development of Orange County during the very era that UC Irvine was taking shape.

The prestigious Center for the Neurobiology of Learning and Memory unites faculty from a variety of backgrounds—biology, psychology, chemistry, cognitive science, pharmacology and genetics—to address brain and memory research. The center's scientists have conducted award-winning research on Alzheimer's disease, false memories, sex differences in memory and a phenomenon called highly superior autobiographical memory—which enables an exlusive number of people to remember their daily lives in extraordinary detail.

▲ *Tom Hayashi and Peggy Woelke, his neighbor and caregiver, visit UCI's Memory Assessment Clinic for his annual Alzheimer's evaluation.*

DETERMINED TO SUCCEED

Nothing goes completely according to plan; successful institutions find ways to deal with the unexpected. UC Irvine's administrators did just that on several occasions. Less than a decade after UCI was founded, Aldrich received a letter from UC President Charles J. Hitch addressed to all UC chancellors. It announced that enrollment calculations for several of the campuses would be adjusted downward due to funding constraints and erroneous calculations. By the end of the 1980s, Hitch said, UC Irvine should expect an enrollment of about 7,500 students

> *"We are, after all, our memories. They are our bridge to the past and to the future."*
>
> —James L. McGaugh
> FOUNDING PROFESSOR OF PSYCHOBIOLOGY
> AND FOUNDING DIRECTOR CENTER FOR THE
> NEUROBIOLOGY OF LEARNING AND MEMORY

▼ *The rapidly expanding research mission in the early 1990s and efforts to improve diversity result in more women and minorities in the labs.*

instead of the planned-for 27,500. "Well, that was a big shock," Aldrich recalled in 1989, noting that meticulous campus planning was based on strong, steady enrollment growth. Aldrich responded with a counterproposal: 12,000 students. He didn't stop there. With ingenuity and resourcefulness, UC Irvine's administrative and faculty leaders continued to grow the university, achieving an enrollment of almost 17,000 students by the late 1980s.

By the early 1990s, the university was riding high. In 1995, UCI was named one of the nation's top 50 research universities, while *U.S. News & World Report* ranked it among the top quartile of national universities. Rowland received the Nobel Prize in chemistry, and Frederick Reines won the Nobel Prize in physics, the first time that two Nobels in different fields were awarded to a single public university in the same year.

A medical school and on-campus hospital had always been part of the university's long-range plans—ideally, in its second decade—but Aldrich and his staff were taken aback when in 1967 the regents approved moving the California College of Medicine, a small, former osteopathic school based in Los Angeles, to UC Irvine.

Although leaders hoped to eventually build a hospital on campus, the California College of Medicine at UC Irvine was quickly affiliated with the existing Orange County Hospital in the city of Orange, 12 miles from campus, to serve as a teaching facility. Eventually, the university acquired Orange County Hospital, assuming care for a large portion of Orange County's indigent patient population.

As his mom runs to hug him, UCI medical student Edward Wu reacts to news that he's "matched" to a residency program at UCLA Medical Center.

Nobel Accomplishments

It seemed like an ordinary Wednesday morning until news broke on October 11, 1995, that lifted UC Irvine to new heights. Word came that Frederick Reines had won the Nobel Prize in physics, along with Martin Perl of Stanford University, while F. Sherwood "Sherry" Rowland would share the Nobel Prize in chemistry with former graduate student Mario J. Molina and German researcher Paul Crutzen.

Reines won for the discovery of the neutrino, an elusive particle that is one of nature's smallest building blocks, while the chemistry prize recognized the discovery that chlorofluorocarbons destroy atmospheric ozone. Chancellor Laurel L. Wilkening described it as the greatest day for UC Irvine since its founding. The next day, huge blue-and-gold banners were draped from the Physical Sciences I and II buildings proclaiming the prizes.

Reines conducted his initial neutrino research in the mid-1950s while at the Los Alamos National Laboratory. He was perhaps the most highly credentialed of the university's founding faculty, and many observers felt his Nobel Prize was long overdue.

▲ *A banner celebrating the Nobel Prizes of F. Sherwood Rowland and Frederick Reines in the physical sciences courtyard, October 1995.*

▶ *F. Sherwood Rowland and graduate student Mario Molina in their chemistry lab.*

▼ *Frederick Reines and mirror image of his guests.*

Irwin Rose (left) receives the Nobel Prize in chemistry from King Carl Gustaf of Sweden during a ceremony at the Concert Hall in Stockholm, December 10, 2004.

Rowland's research was a homegrown effort and brought the university wide acclaim. His and Moliana's ozone papers were initially disputed by many scientists and policymakers, and the two men persevered for many years before their theory earned international acceptance. Rowland was motivated by deep concern for the environmental disaster that could be wrought by ozone depletion. He continued to frequent his lab in the Physical Sciences I Building—renamed Rowland Hall in 1998—long after his official retirement.

The discovery "was about more than just stratospheric ozone," Donald Blake, a chemistry professor who worked with Rowland, told the *Los Angeles Times* after Rowland's death in 2012. "It was about the whole environment and the realization that something we can do in California could have effects somewhere else in the world. It was the start of the global era of the environment."

Rowland's research on ozone depletion led to the 1991 founding of UCI's Earth system science department, today recognized as one of the nation's most influential academic units devoted to studying the Earth as a system. It was an early leader in the focus on global climate change. It houses the W.M. Keck Carbon Cycle Accelerator Mass Spectrometry Facility, the first in the United States dedicated exclusively to research on greenhouse gases and global warming. Faculty and students study topics such as oil spills, climate change and drought. Recent research has demonstrated the unsustainable depletion of groundwater in California's Central Valley, the impact of urban green spaces on global warming, and the irreversible disappearance of ice sheets around the world.

UC Irvine's third faculty Nobel winner was Irwin Rose, who won the prize in chemistry in 2004 along with Aaron Ciechanover and Avram Hershko of the Israel Institute of Technology, for the discovery of the ubiquitin protein. He made the breakthrough while at the Fox Chase Cancer Center in Philadelphia. Rose retired to Orange County in 1997, accepting a special appointment as researcher emeritus at UC Irvine and continuing his work.

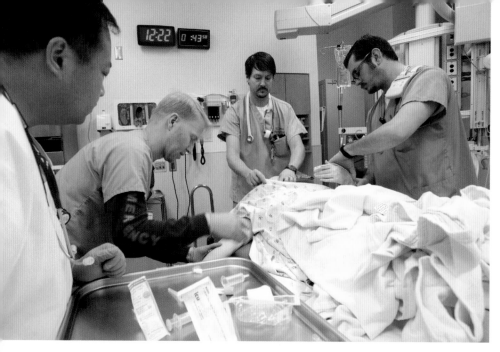

◀ A team at UC Irvine Douglas Hospital, Orange County's only Level 1 Trauma Center, draws blood from a patient.

▼ Computers and tablets make it easier for doctors and nurses to receive lab and X-ray results.

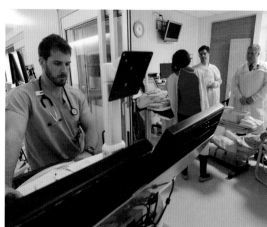

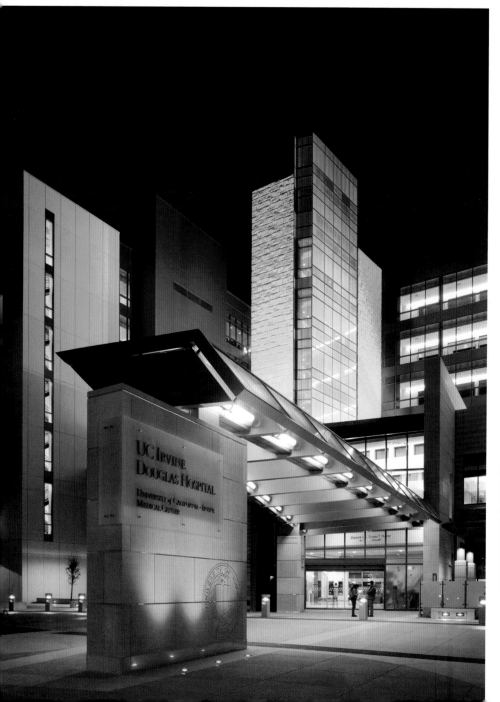

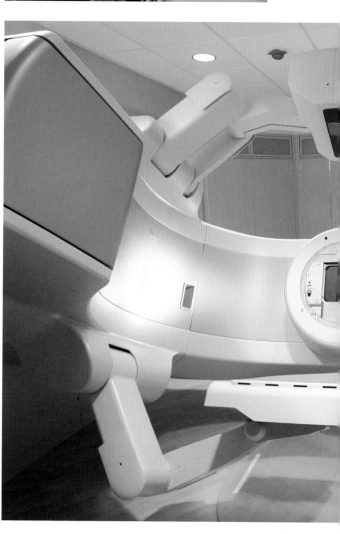

◀ *Warren Wiechmann, assistant clinical professor of emergency medicine and associate dean of instructional technologies, supervises the integration of Google Glass into the four-year medical school program.*

For many years, campus leaders struggled to cover the hospital's costs while raising the quality of care and improving the facilities. Dreams of an on-campus hospital faded, but the resolve to make the medical school into one of the nation's finest did not.

In the late 1980s, an outpatient medical pavilion opened on campus, while the medical faculty earned acclaim for innovative medical advances, such as discovering a segment of DNA that could predict the onset of Huntington's disease, pioneering the use of PET scanning in psychiatric research and identifying tumor suppressor cells, which play a major role in cancer development. The school is renowned across the country for its technological savvy. It was the first to equip all incoming medical students with iPads containing the entire first-year curriculum and diagnostic tools. Google Glass has been incorporated to allow students to securely broadcast patient care for training purposes. Future doctors can view themselves through the patients' eyes, experience patient care from the patients' perspective, and learn from that information how to become more empathic and engaged physicians. The sophisticated Medical Education Simulation Center is outfitted with lifelike computer-controlled mannequins that react to treatments.

In 2001, the regents approved $235 million to construct a new hospital, which opened in 2009; it was officially dedicated as Douglas Hospital at UC Irvine Medical Center in 2010. The 411-bed facility is the only university hospital—and the only Level I Trauma Center—in the county. Spanning 52 acres in the heart of Orange, the medical center is now regarded as a jewel among the region's healthcare resources, consistently ranked among America's Best Hospitals by *U.S. News & World Report*. The complex includes the Chao Family Comprehensive Cancer Center, one of the few facilities in California designated by the National Cancer Institute as a comprehensive cancer center, as well as a renowned program in geriatrics.

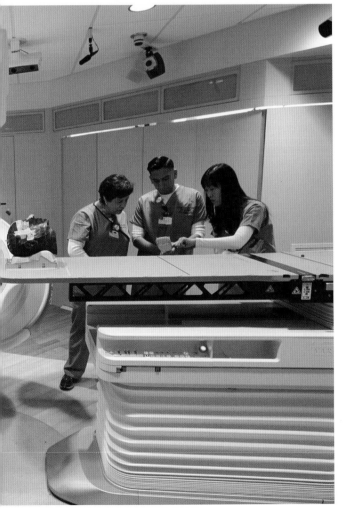

◀ *Diagnostic and treatment facilities at Douglas Hospital feature the latest technology.*

► *UC Irvine School of Law houses clinics—such as immigration and family violence—that serve the community. Pro bono work is a core value.*

The best and the brightest

Universities must continually confront challenges, such as the economic downturn that began in 2007, which led to steep fee increases throughout California's public university system. But, said Gillman: "Staying strong and moving forward relentlessly, even in the face of those challenges, is a hallmark of the place. This institution did a lot of heroic work during the 2007–2008 economic downturn, but it wasn't purely defensive work. It decided it would create a world-class law school at exactly that time and did it better than anyone's ever done it."

Founding leadership had always intended to create a law school. The Academic Senate approved a proposal in 1990, but budget woes shelved it. Ten years later, the regents accepted a revamped plan.

> *"We have built this campus and assembled amazing faculty, because human beings only reach their full potential when exposed to the best that has ever been thought, created or discovered."*
>
> —**Howard Gillman**
> Chancellor, 2014–

◄ *Newly minted lawyers Yimeng Dou, left, and Sam Lam from the inaugural class give each other a celebratory high-five during a swearing-in ceremony, 2012.*

▼ *Catherine Fisk, Chancellor's Professor of Law, codirects the Center in Law, Society and Culture.*

▼ *Renowned constitutional expert Erwin Chemerinsky, dean, Distinguished Professor of Law, and Raymond Pryke Professor of First Amendment Law, leads a student tour.*

The first proposal "never really got traction, partly because it was described as something to help the university," said Michael V. Drake, UCI's chancellor from 2005–2014. "We decided to turn this around a bit and make this something that would help the community; something we could do for the people of the region."

Erwin Chemerinsky, a renowned and much-cited constitutional law scholar, was appointed dean, and the school welcomed its inaugural class in 2009, becoming the first public law school to open in California in more than 40 years and an immediate success. Within a few years, the faculty was ranked ninth in the nation in scholarly impact. In 2012, the school, in only its third year, was ranked seventh for its scholarly impact, while the first graduating class in 2012 achieved a high rate of clerkships, ranking third in the nation. In spring, 2014, the UC Irvine School of Law earned accreditation at the earliest possible time allowable under American Bar Association rules.

▼ *Eager space-age engineering students take their seats for Dean Robert Saunders' lecture in 1965. Four years later, Neil Armstrong takes his giant leap for mankind.*

▶ *National Fuel Cell Research Center Associate Director Jack Brouwer is a proponent of clean-burning hydrogen.*

THE NEXT HALF-CENTURY

In 2012, California voters passed a referendum increasing taxes in support of public education. With the state emerging from the Great Recession, the tax stabilized higher education. But it does not guarantee the growth of the campus. Only the people at UC Irvine can do that, said Gillman in 2013.

"Our future is once again in our hands," Gillman said. "It means that we have to draw on that great history and be creative and think of new ways over the next 10 years to expand the impact we have on students, on knowledge creation and on the world. It's going to take thinking in new ways." Echoing the sentiments of Chancellor Drake, he added: "Being bold and innovative is the only option any institution has at this stage. Our strategic advantage is that we've always done it this way, so we're not deterred by a new set of challenges. We're going to figure out how to do it our way."

The 50th anniversary dawns on a university awash in accolades. The Paul Merage School of Business boasts MBA programs that rank among the best in the world as well as the highest rate of employment within three months of graduating, according to the *Financial Times*. The School of Education has evolved into one of the university's strongest research faculties.

▲ *Engineering Hall is a hub for research and an award-winning building for its sustainable design.*

The Henry Samueli School of Engineering focuses on preparing students for the demands of the 21st century with programs in the science and engineering of human health, environmental science and engineering, sustainable energy and transportation systems, and communications and information technology. In 1987, the school opened the state's first program in environmental engineering—combining courses in engineering, biological sciences and social sciences. The California Institute for Telecommunications and Information Technology, a joint project with UC San Diego that was created in 2000, develops information technology-based innovations in a multidisciplinary environment,

▶ *A chemical engineering researcher at work.*

▼ *A lecture sponsored by Institute for Genomics and Bioinformatics illustrates the intersection of life and computational sciences.*

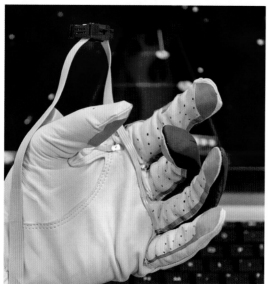

▲ *A glove, outfitted with finger sensors, generates musical notes and encourages patients with stroke or head injuries to exercise by creating music.*

integrating academic research with industry experience. Groundbreaking work in biomedical engineering has included Music Glove, which features sensors that link a robotic glove to a computer and allows stroke rehab patients to play songs on Guitar Hero by tapping their fingers together.

The Sue & Bill Gross Hall: A CIRM Institutue, home of UCI's stem cell research center, opened in 2010 as one of 12 centers funded by the California Institute for Regenerative Medicine. Work at the center is aimed at harnessing the therapeutic potential of stem cell science to cure human disease and heal injury. The program has attracted some of the brightest scientists in the field. In 2002, UC Irvine neurobiologist Hans Keirstead was the first to develop a human embryonic stem cell therapy that restored greater mobility in animal models with spinal cord injury. These cutting-edge biomedical research programs build on UC Irvine's longstanding strengths in developmental biology.

Today, UC Irvine retains the exuberance of its founding fathers, Gillman noted. "Part of that is reflective of that confidence of youth—that because we're young and ambitious, we can't stop moving forward," he said. "Even if there are hard decisions to make, we're still going to make great things happen."

Leaders envision an enrollment of 32,000 students in the coming years, with about one-quarter of those being graduate students. With robust

▲ *Aileen Anderson (left) and technician Gaby Funes culture human stem cells in the biosafety cabinet.*

summer programs and international student enrollment, UC Irvine has continued to expand despite the economic downturn. More than ever, current leaders say, the values of UC Irvine's founders—perseverance, flexibility, innovation and the commitment to excellence—should be summoned for the march into the future.

"It's as important for us to celebrate the last 50 years as it is to imagine the next 50 years," Gillman said. "The point of the celebration is to inspire us to greater heights and to motivate us to make even stronger contributions to the well-being of the world. If we do that, we will be faithful to all of those people 50 years ago who had a dream. We owe it to all of them to set our sights high."

▼ *Brian Cummings (right), with PhD student Eric Gold, studies fluorescent images in brain injury research.*

◀ *Student at early computer, 1967.*

◀◀ *A student experiments with a pen that creates 3-D structures in a Calit2 lab run by informatics professor Geoffrey Bowker who brings together researchers from computer science, engineering, design, anthropology, philosophy and art to develop techniques for responsible technological innovation.*

▲ *Students collaborate on a calculation outside the UCI Student Center.*

▶ *Computer Facility Director Robert Gordon confers with Charlene Newnes, 1968.*

▶▶ *Constructing scientific models: a research worker with gloved hands under a fume hood.*

▶ *Today, extracurricular learning through clubs and cultural activities are a large part of the student experience, and computer mobility means any food court can become a study hall.*

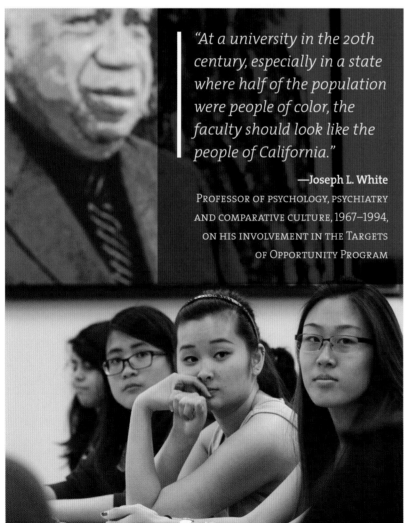

"At a university in the 20th century, especially in a state where half of the population were people of color, the faculty should look like the people of California."

—Joseph L. White
PROFESSOR OF PSYCHOLOGY, PSYCHIATRY AND COMPARATIVE CULTURE, 1967–1994, ON HIS INVOLVEMENT IN THE TARGETS OF OPPORTUNITY PROGRAM

chapter 4

"you make your own future here"

The Sound of Music played in theaters, race riots plagued American cities and The Beatles' "Yesterday" topped music charts when the inaugural students of UC Irvine strolled up a dusty path to attend classes on October 4, 1965. Women wore pageboy haircuts and knee-length skirts while men dressed in slacks and shirts with some sporting ties. Of the 1,589 enrolled on that day, 958 were freshmen. They were barely 18, and yet they were already mavericks.

▶ *Graduating members of the Class of 1966 gather in Gateway Commons for commencement dinner address by mathematics professor Bernard R. Gelbaum, left.*

◀ *First day of classes, October 4, 1965.*

4

These students created the first identity of the nascent school. They plunged their hands in fresh cement and left their imprint—a spirit of independence, ambition and social consciousness that still characterizes the student body half a century later.

Eight new buildings hugged one half of William Pereira's Ring Mall on opening day. Inside classrooms, smells of fresh carpet and paint greeted students. A trailer across the street housed the bookstore.

Although many commuted, university leaders intended to provide shelter to as many students as possible on or near campus. They scrambled to welcome that first batch of pillow-toting students. The beds in Mesa Court were delivered at midnight on the eve of move-in day. Cognizant that it would not be easy to foster a rich social climate on a campus started from scratch, Chancellor Daniel G. Aldrich Jr. and Pereira chose to avoid the massive multistory dorms that were popular in that era. Mesa Court's 500 residents were housed in 10 two-story cottages meant to foster close friendships and self-government.

▲ *Ellene Sumner, housing and food director, checks out the rugs for Mesa Court residences, 1965.*

▼ *With a definite frontier feel, Irvine Town Center trailers, from left, house a post office, the university interfaith center, a Bank of America branch and UCI University Book Store. Only the post office remains.*

◀ *Students make use of the lawn at Mesa Court, 1966.*

▼ *Couches in the lobby of Bahia, one of 10 two-story residence halls in Mesa Court, provide a comfy spot for reading. Housing units accommodating 50 students sequester men and women in separate buildings in 1965.*

Student life in 1965 had its ups and downs, recalled Charlie Brande, a freshman at the time who would later return to coach the men's and women's volleyball teams. "There was a uniqueness about it, and I think that bonded us together," he said. "The trees around the ring were little twigs. I took an information and computer sciences class, but there were no computers. One day, it rained so hard that it flooded all the way around the dorm, and we couldn't get out."

Nutritional sustenance required a long trek to the Commons cafeteria. However, students who became ill could rely on school nurse Norma Grundy, who operated a clinic from one wing of Crawford Hall but was known to make house calls to the dorms. Those who desired off-campus living gravitated to Balboa Island. It remained a popular area in which to live and play until the late 1980s, when soaring rents chased away most collegians.

▼ *Small classes frequently meet in outdoor areas like the court outside the Fine Arts Building.*

University leaders were quick to organize intramural sports and other activities to engage students. A Campus Hall sock hop, Halloween costume dance and pancake-eating contest were among the first social events of the new university. In November, professors Clayton Garrison and Colin Slim and choreographer Eugene Loring presented a student production of *Little Mary Sunshine* to a sellout crowd on campus. Catherine Kerr, wife of UC President Clark Kerr, traveled from her home in Berkeley to support the effort.

The Bohemian Life

The Irvine Meadows residential trailer park opened on the west side of campus in fall 1979. Irvine Meadows was a cheap, funky housing alternative that quickly became a student favorite. At the first student-housing mobile home park in the country, residents enjoyed rental fees of only $130 a month and decorated the exterior of their homes with flags, lawn furniture and potted plants. The 80-unit park was also home to rabbits, cats and goats, and residents could hear the forlorn cries of coyotes at night. Students from around the campus celebrated the end of each quarter with a party at Irvine Meadows and competed fiercely for the few homes that became available each spring.

But all good things must come to an end. In 1999, the university announced the park would close, giving students a full five years to come to grips with the fact. In July 2004, despite residents' pleas and protestations—and even a few words of regret from university administrators—close it did. The last straggler turned off the lights on August 3. The university later designated the land for parking, leaving students with only one possible rejoinder. In the words of singer Joni Mitchell: "They paved paradise and put up a parking lot."

> *"The park was location central for me: I had a short walk to the original gym and track and an even shorter walk to the fine arts department. There was no power nor bathroom at the park (two bathrooms were built around 1975), but you couldn't beat the rent."*
>
> —Michael Sabatino '79
> THREE-TIME ALL AMERICAN AND NCAA DIVISION II POLE-VAULT CHAMPION, AND MEMBER OF THE 1975 NCAA DIVISION II CHAMPION TRACK TEAM

▲ *Michael Sabatino '79 at Irvine Meadows trailer park.*

The first intercollegiate athletic event took place 12 days after classes began when the men's water polo team crushed Cal Poly Pomona, 22–6, before a robust turnout: 900 of the 1,598 student population attended. That first event made it clear that the campus was sorely in need of a mascot. Aldrich had already floated some ideas, including roadrunner, unicorn, seahawk and golden bison.

Freshman water polo players Pat Glasgow and Bob Ernst were not impressed, feeling UC Irvine needed something inimitable. They were fans of the popular

▶ *A live anteater on campus? Nobody knows how he got there.*

▶ *A student enjoys down time at UCI Student Center with bronze Peter, a gift from the Class of 2003.*

Johnny Hart comic strip *B.C.*, which featured an anteater. They proposed the Anteater name to some buddies, including Schuyler Hadley Bassett III. Sold on the notion, Bassett began blitzing the campus with pro-Anteater literature, explaining to students that "Zot!" was the sound the animal makes when attacking its prey. He even established his own unofficial fraternity, Zeta Omega Tau—ZOT.

There were few mature upperclassmen to temper such freshman enthusiasm, he recalled. "The freshmen—we ruled the campus," Bassett said. "We were the big men on campus. We were resolved that we had to have a silly name." Students voted for a mascot on November 30, 1965. Anteater emerged victorious with 55.9 percent of the vote, which convincingly beat out the runner-up "none of these." The charter students had indeed made their mark. The selection of Anteater made the national Huntley-Brinkley TV newscast and the pages of *Sports Illustrated*.

◀ *Coach Al Irwin talks to his water polo team before an October 1965 match, the first intercollegiate athletic event at UCI.*

103

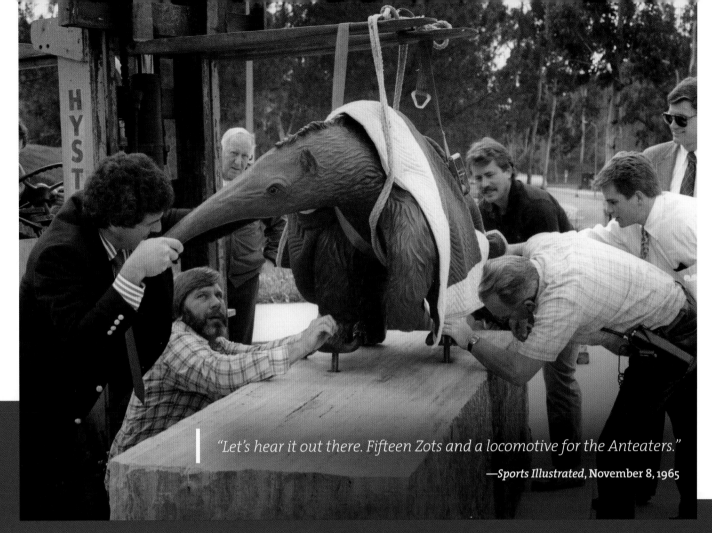

> "Let's hear it out there. Fifteen Zots and a locomotive for the Anteaters."
>
> —*Sports Illustrated*, November 8, 1965

No doubt about it: Peter the Anteater is the face of UCI. And what a face it is! Over the years, multiple makeovers take the mascot from oversized fur ball to buff anteater with biceps. Opposite page clockwise from top left, Peter gets a hug from Mickey Mouse, 1988; space-alien anteater on rollerblades, 1994; current incarnation, 2005; laid-back-dude anteater, 1980; and plush version, 1999. This page, workers in 1987 install 350-pound bronze anteater by sculptor Billy Fitzgerald outside the Bren Events Center. The sculpture, a gift from the Class of 1987, is an often-photographed icon, especially at commencement.

> "In 1974, UCI's Administration asked the Associated Students Council to revisit the mascot's name. After several spirited meetings a formal vote was held but the outcome wasn't in doubt. We were determined to keep the Anteater as UCI's campus symbol. Forty-one years later our affirmation remains in place. 'Zot!' to that!"
>
> —Mark Brickley '75

◀ *Anthill Pub and Grille gives students*
▼ *a venue to discuss everything from*
   Plato to politics over pilsner.

Today, "Zot!" is synonymous with UC Irvine, with "Zot!" Alerts, "Zot!" Mail and a campus store called the Zot-n-Go. In 2010, students named the spirit organization Antourage. Home athletic events take place in 'Eater Nation, and a favorite campus gathering spot is the Anthill Pub & Grille. Anteaters have tutored US presidents past and present in the proper execution of the "Zot!" hand sign.

FORGING A STUDENT GOVERNMENT

Not everyone approved of the Anteater as the face of UC Irvine, but—at least publicly—Aldrich kept mum. He had an uncanny understanding of young minds. Throughout the difficult and exhilarating early years, he permitted students to express themselves while keeping watch on the university's emerging reputation. UC Irvine was born in an era of heated civil rights and antiwar activism. Aldrich forged exceptionally close relationships with the charter classes.

On the eve of his inauguration, May 20, 1966, students stayed up all night stringing pom-pom streamers from the library's top floor. Dressed in suits and ties, dresses and elbow-length gloves, the teens celebrated with the chancellor and presented him with a gift: a clock. During the inauguration, physics major Mark Massachia praised the campus's social, political and academic climate: "UCI has what is probably the greatest degree of student freedom of just about any other campus in California."

Polls became commonplace as students worked to lay down the characteristics and codes of behavior that would dictate campus life. One committee wrote an honor code and another a constitution. By the spring, the UC Irvine Student Assembly had formed, but it was tough going for the first elected leaders. The 1967–1968 president and vice president resigned their positions midway through that year, citing student apathy.

Integral to the formation of campus protocols and traditions was the student-operated media. The independent student newspaper *Spectrum* was founded one week after classes began, and the first issue appeared on

▲ *Chancellor Dan, as he is fondly known, talks frequently with students. For his inauguration in 1966, students stay up most of the night decorating the Library-Administration building (now Langson Library) with brightly colored pom-poms.*

October 20 featuring a story lamenting the lack of parking. *Spectrum* lasted one year and was followed by the brief appearance of the *Tongue* in 1966, which had a *Mad Magazine* flavor and gained notoriety for helping to defeat the university's first proposed constitution. The *Anthill* published for a few years before the *New University* newspaper was founded in 1968. The name of *New University* was chosen as a reminder that UC Irvine would continually reinvent itself to become stronger, better—"the constant state of a pioneering spirit," explained former Vice Chancellor of Student Affairs Manuel Gomez, who worked at the university for 38 years before retiring in 2010.

While publishing was unpredictable in those early years, the university's radio station got off the ground in fall 1969 and never looked back. Radio KUCI was the students' stab at legitimacy; they had been broadcasting illegally from the dorms for weeks before applying for a license. Operating on a 10-watt signal, the official KUCI staffers set up shop in a Physical Sciences building closet and debuted with a program entitled *Problems of the World Solved Tonight*. The inaugural deejay chose "Sugar, Sugar" as the first song. The station thrived. By the university's silver anniversary, it had grown to a 24-hour operation staffed by 120 student volunteers. Now broadcasting at more than 200 watts on 88.9 FM and streaming on the web, KUCI can be heard across Orange County and beyond.

FREEDOM RINGS ON RING MALL

The rise of student-operated media was essential to the charter classes' solemn belief in freedom of speech—and students were quick to exercise that right. The first large demonstration occurred at Gateway Plaza in January 1967, when more than 1,500 UC Irvine students, faculty and staff protested Clark Kerr's dismissal by the UC regents. As UC president, Kerr had been criticized for appearing overly tolerant of student unrest. The 1967 yearbook editors described the event's significance: "A new generation of students would emerge, impatient with the status quo, committed to righting old wrongs through direct action and, in the process, shocking their elders and shaking institutions." They dedicated the yearbook to Kerr.

In 1968, demonstrators once again took to Ring Mall when three popular humanities professors were denied tenure and released. About 500 of the 4,100-person student body protested the administration's decision. After a march on the Administration Building, 40 students began a five-day "live-in" at the Writing Center. "The aim, of course, was to provoke the chancellor into calling in the police to remove the demonstrators forcibly," noted UC Irvine historian Samuel Clyde McCulloch. "However, Aldrich didn't take the bait. He informed the students: 'As long as [you] are not obstructive or destructive, so be it.'" The protest was resolved when the administration agreed to rewrite its policies on the appeals process for dismissed faculty.

▲ *KUCI broadcasts and web streams alternative music, interview segments and athletic events to campus and community.*

▶ *Chancellor Aldrich speaks to students*
▼ *protesting the firing of UC President Clark Kerr on January 23, 1967. Budget cuts are also a subject of contention.*

> "UCI was born in a rich but tumultuous time of vaulted ambition, but also anger, disappointment and cynicism about the war in Vietnam. Big Dan (Aldrich) was a rock."
>
> —**Keith Nelson**
> FOUNDING PROFESSOR OF HISTORY

▲ *A student tries his hand at a UCI bowtie at The Hill, UCI's bookstore.*

▶ *UCI Student Center is a popular spot for students, faculty and staff alike to kick back with laptops.*

The Fight for a Student Center

▲ *The bell tower at the student center rings on the hour, a gift from Class of 2010.*

A student center was not a high priority for UCI's charter students. The campus opened without a union, although the Commons dining hall served as an informal gathering spot. In 1967, the Campus Union Planning Committee was formed to discuss building a student center, but special funding was required. Four times in five years, from 1970–1974, referenda to increase student fees (as low as $6 per quarter) in support of a student center failed at the polls. On the fifth try, in 1975, the referendum succeeded.

The University Center opened in January 1981 only to be expanded in 1989 and renamed the Student Center. The renovated center, 1991 yearbook editors proclaimed, "has ... given UCI the feeling of a 'real' school." Heavily used and straining to contain a growing student body, the center was again expanded and remodeled in 2007. It now features meeting rooms, an auditorium, an arcade room, computer labs, two food courts and a completely student-run Starbucks that has the notoriety of being one of the busiest in the nation. A place to meet, eat and nap—it is truly the heart of the campus.

◀ *Completed in 2007 and crowned with a bronze anteater, the UCI Student Center is a hub for campus activities.*

▼ *Food Court in student center doubles as study hall.*

▲ *Coffee drinks at the student-run Starbucks keep the campus community caffeinated. At finals time, the line wraps around the facility.*

◀ *Fast-food vendors serve the eat-and-run needs of students.*

Aldrich remained a steady hand in the turbulent 1960s, toeing a delicate line between supporting student rights and convincing university neighbors that he was not ceding authority to a mob of left-leaning radicals.

"Staunchly conservative Orange County kept a suspicious eye on its new UC campus for any signs of 'rebellion' or 'radicalism,'" McCulloch noted.

Other UC campuses experienced far more disruptive activism in the 1960s, and the protests sometimes spilled over. In May 1969, the Berkeley People's Park incident incited 33 UC Irvine students to barge into a chancellor's administrative advisory council meeting with demands to discuss the Berkeley situation. Aldrich defused the situation, and a headline in the May 26 *Los Angeles Times* declared: "Dialogue Minus Violence: UCI Builds a Tradition."

Today, the area near Langson Library, the Student Center and Ring Mall has emerged as the campus free-speech zone. On any given day, students can find someone to discuss student fee increases, fighting in the Middle East, the nation's use of fossil fuels or any number of issues. "UCI has a very different style of activism," said Megan C. Braun, who served as president of the Associated Students of UCI in 2009–2010 and was also UCI's first Rhodes Scholar. "You would never see someone setting a fire in a dumpster at Irvine. Yes, there are rallies, but they aren't destructive. It's purposeful activism, and it unfolds in a very different way. It may look passive from the outside, but it's more focused on issues and solutions."

▲ *Delta Delta Delta sorority is one of many themed housing facilities at Arroyo Vista.*

▼ *Tri-Delt sisters host a group study session leading up to finals, March 2014.*

A SHOCKING AMOUNT OF FUN

By UCI's 10th birthday, administrators were more concerned about fostering a sense of community among students than extinguishing overzealous rallies. After the university's second year, the student body was either unable or too disinterested to publish a yearbook. The revived yearbook in 1976 hinted at difficult times: an unpopular war, Watergate and high unemployment.

Students in the 1970s did not resemble those who traversed the campus a decade earlier. These students wore their hair long, lived in coed dorms and sought independence. Observed McCulloch: "At UCI, as at most other universities, rules governing the personal lives of students were out of fashion."

But the university was, in fact, creating a tableau of traditions and clubs. By 1979, there were more than 180 campus organizations, ranging from academically themed (Pre-Law Society) to purely fun (Frisbee Club) to socially conscious (Alliance for Survival, an anti-nuclear arms group). Many clubs launched their own annual events, such as the Engineering Club's popular Engineering Week. "We had more clubs at UC Irvine than almost any other university," Gomez said. "That says the spirit of the student culture is manifested by student leaders creating their own organizations."

The Greek system took root as well. When the campus opened, Aldrich had heeded advice from the Student Senate and Academic Senate to ban national social organizations from campus. In 1972, however, the Supreme Court of the United States ruled that prohibiting the existence of national organizations on college or university campuses violated the First Amendment. Aldrich appointed a faculty-student-staff committee to advise him, and the group recommended that three fraternities and three sororities be admitted. The first rush week was held in 1974. By 1986, 12 percent of students were members. In 1994, some of the Greek groups eagerly established their own houses in the Arroyo Vista housing complex, which allowed for "themed" residences. Today, the university's Greek life boasts impressive records of philanthropy and community service.

UCI's sororities and fraternities join forces annually for Greek Songfest. Ticket sales in 2010 benefit Orange County Food Bank.

Fraternities and sororities also provided the support needed to establish campuswide events, such as Wayzgoose, one of the oldest and largest university social gatherings, conceived as a way to liven up the campus social scene. Debuting in 1972, the medieval-themed fair features jesters, baroque rock groups, madrigal choirs, folk dancers, games and crafts. The festival eventually merged with Celebrate UCI, the university's annual open house. The major social event of the fall was founded in 1996 as an Oktoberfest celebration. It was repackaged in 2001 as the hipper Shocktoberfest and now includes a street festival on Mesa Road featuring free food, a Midnight Magic party at the Bren Events Center to introduce the season's men's and women's basketball teams (touted as the West Coast's largest basketball kickoff event), a concert and, to stretch the fun just a bit longer, an Aftershock dance party.

▲ *Shocktoberfest, an undergraduate student tradition, marks the start of basketball practice season.*

▶ *Students rock the Bren Events Center at Shocktoberfest concert.*

EVERY STUDENT UNDER THE RAINBOW

Many campus events are linked to celebrations of ethnic diversity that began in the late 1970s with recognitions of black history and Martin Luther King Jr. The university's early leaders were eager to promote diversity. Joseph L. White, a child psychologist who began his career at California State University, Long Beach, came to UC Irvine in 1969 to teach psychology and comparative culture. While at Cal State Long Beach he helped found the Educational Opportunity Program in California, designed to attract more minority students to the state's public universities.

▼ *Developing a sense of shared community over pasta.*

▲ *From left, Aldrich, Robert Weaver and ASUCI President Ron Ridgle greet each other in 1969 before Weaver's address on the 101ˢᵗ anniversary of UC. As Secretary of Housing and Urban Development in the Johnson administration, Weaver is the first black cabinet member.*

▼ *Students celebrate during a Welcome Week ceremony.*

The launch of the program at Irvine, in 1968, brought a contingent of about 100 minority students to campus—a distinct improvement upon the class of 1965–1966, which featured one African American student, Ron Ridgle. He became ASUCI president in May 1968 and supported a controversial decision to invite political activist Eldridge Cleaver to a panel discussion on "America as a Racist Culture."

By 1971, 3.5 percent of UC Irvine's student body identified as minorities. University officials were sensitive to underrepresented students and, in what was a prescient decision, created the Cross-Cultural Center in 1975 to address their personal, social, cultural and academic needs. "The student-body-elected officials were mostly white then," White recalled. "I think the university felt minority students needed a center to address their concerns. It's a place where they could express their goals and ideas."

The center, housed in a temporary building across Ring Mall from the School of Humanities, became the first of its kind in the UC system and emerged as a model for universities across the country. In its early years, "The Cross" umbrella included the Afrikan Student Union, Movimiento Estudiantil Chicano de Aztlán (M.E.Ch.A.), the Asian Pacific Student Association, Alyansa ng mga Kababayan and the American Indian Student Association. Shortly after it opened, the Cross-Cultural Center unveiled a mural painted by UC Irvine students depicting significant historical people and events in California's minority communities. Murals became part of the center's

"*If only every student at UCI could walk through the 'Cross' and take with them what so many students take with them ... they would somehow be touched by the people, programs or the place itself.*"

—**Corina Espinoza**
CROSS-CULTURAL CENTER DIRECTOR, 1990–1999

identity, as did the Rainbow Festival, established in 1984 to celebrate cultural and ethnic diversity. UC Irvine's inaugural Rainbow Festival was themed "Many Faces, Many Dreams," which describes the university today.

Ethnic diversity in the faculty was harder to achieve. In the mid-1980s, White and several associates formed a program, entitled Targets of Opportunity designed to attract underrepresented ethnic minority faculty—African Americans and Hispanics in particular. "We felt that at a university in the 20th century, especially in a state where half the population were people of color, the faculty should look like the people of California," White said.

The program brought in a handful of new faculty, but that wasn't enough to satisfy students hungry for classes on cultural diversity. In 1991,

▲ *The Cross-Cultural Center provides experiences in extracurricular learning.*

▶ *Olive Tree Initiative participant visits memorial to victims of suicide attack at Haifa, Israel.*

▼ *Students gather at Temple Mount/Haram al-Sharif in the Old City of Jerusalem.*

The Olive Tree Initiative, founded at UC Irvine in 2007, provides for open, respectful discourse on conflict in the Middle East among students of diverse religious, political and cultural backgrounds. It has expanded to three additional UC campuses and won recognition from the UC Office of the President and the Orange County Human Relations Commission. Director Daniel Wehrenfennig participates in White House roundtable discussions on peace.

◀ *Munib Masri of Nablus hosts Olive Tree Initiative students in his home.*

◀ *An observation point on a tour of the Golan Heights offers a photo opportunity.*

▲ *The Western Wall or Wailing Wall in the Old City of Jerusalem tells many stories.*

117

▼ *Farmers' market at University Center sells ethnic greens and other foods, March 2014.*

▲ *Students rest on roots of the iconic Moreton Bay Fig tree that anchors the center of Aldrich Park.*

several student organizations established the Ethnic Students Coalition Against Prejudicial Education to press for ethnic studies programs. The campaign reached a boiling point in 1993 when Asian American students held a 35-day rotational hunger strike to call attention to their demands. Administrators reached an agreement with the students to add three faculty positions and a director of Asian American Studies. Eventually, two interdisciplinary minors were added in African American studies and Chicano/Latino studies. Today, the UCI ADVANCE program oversees a cadre of equity advisers in each school that encourages ethnic and gender diversity in academic hiring.

Student diversity is celebrated on the Irvine campus on a daily basis, through clubs and social activities, ethnic food booths (shouts of "Boba, $2" ring out regularly), festivals, dances, classes and speeches. Religious diversity also thrives, with as many as 50 religious groups on campus. By UC Irvine's silver anniversary in 1990, Asian American students formed the largest ethnic contingent on campus, at roughly 48 percent.

'Eater nation comes of age

Adolescence is awkward. It's a time of unruly growth and change and self-doubt. UC Irvine in the fall of 1980—its 15th anniversary—was still trying to find its identity as a community. Enrollment topped 10,000 by the 1979–1980 academic year, and students grumbled about long lines at the bookstore and library. They competed for seats in some classrooms. More than 80 percent lived off campus at the start of the decade, and the campus had not managed to shake off its reputation as having a dull social atmosphere. Editors in the 1987 yearbook lamented, "At UCI, studying is the predominant activity." Historian McCulloch noted that the pioneering spirit of the university's first graduating classes had faded away. "Students were more pragmatic," he observed. "There was an increasingly competitive academic atmosphere, which focused on escalating costs for education and the very real concern of finding a job after graduation."

When Jack W. Peltason took office as chancellor in 1984, he noted that campus construction was a constant, visible reminder that UC Irvine was still in its formative stage. "UCI is a gangly adolescent, and we are having to endure some adolescent problems," Peltason told students. "You are going to school at a construction site." UCI's second chancellor thought long and hard about how to enrich student life and campus culture and wouldn't give up until he succeeded, establishing public lectures and arts displays and expanding athletic programs, said Thomas A. Parham, who was appointed vice chancellor of student affairs in 2011, and who was a UC Irvine student from 1975–1977. "Jack had a vision that universities should be 24-hour places and not just a place where you study and go home or teach and go home," Parham said. "That flavor, that value, began to permeate the campus."

After 16 years, students and alumni realized that although they lacked a football team, they could still have a homecoming celebration. Enthusiasm for Anteater sports was mounting, a turn of events the university's founders had long hoped for.

▼ *"Boba, $2!" is a common refrain around Ring Mall. It's a favorite fundraiser for student groups.*

▶ *From left, Director of Athletics Wayne Crawford and the UCI coaching staff, April 1965: Dick Skeen (tennis), Duvall Hecht (crew), Ray Thornton (intramural), Dan Rogers (basketball) and Albert Irwin (aquatics).*

In 1965, founding athletic director Wayne Crawford had formed programs in basketball, golf, tennis, swimming, water polo, sailing and crew—all men's teams. Crawford established a community group called the Big I Boosters, and Orange County residents pitched in to get several teams off the ground. Duvall Hecht, who had won a gold medal in the 1956 Olympics in rowing, lobbied Aldrich for crew as an intercollegiate sport, noting that beautiful Newport Bay was perfect for racing. With the support of a group of local men who were onetime competitive rowers, a boathouse was constructed at Shellmaker Island in Upper Newport Bay and a team was launched with "40 inexperienced men," according to the university's inaugural yearbook. The program went on to produce several Olympians.

Men's water polo made a splash from the start and remained a standout program for much of its first 50 years. Inaugural coach Al Irwin stocked his first team with four Junior College All-Americans, and the team finished the season boasting a national ranking. In 1970–1971, the team won their first NCAA championship.

"When I came into UCI, we had a terrible pool," recalled former coach Ted Newland, who joined the program in 1968. "We used to call it the toilet. It was small and shallow and narrow. I had to travel with my team to find a good pool to work out in. It was a unique start." Newland went on to lead the team to six NCAA championships in water polo and six second-place finishes. The school finally got a new pool in 2000.

Aquatics Coach Al Irwin (left) and Director of Athletics Wayne Crawford at pool site.

▲ UCI crews hold a brisk workout on the course at Lido Channel.

Anteaters in Gold, Silver and Bronze

Jennifer Chandler made history in 1976 when she became the first UC Irvine student to win an Olympic gold medal. Chandler won her medal in springboard diving the same year that UC Irvine student Greg Louganis won a silver in platform diving. Louganis went on to win four gold medals at the 1984 and 1988 games. Over the years, 37 students and nine coaches have participated in the Olympics as competitors, earning six gold medals, 16 silver medals and one bronze. Twelve Anteaters competed in the 1984 Olympic Games in Los Angeles. Several other students and coaches have also coached in the Olympics. John Morgan ranks as UCI's most decorated Olympic athlete with 15 medals in swimming from the 1984 and 1992 Paralympic Games.

▶ Greg Louganis '81.

▼ UCI alums and members of the 2004 US water polo Olympic team, from left, Ryan Bailey '06, Jeff Powers '03, Omar Amr '96, Genai Kerr and Dan Klatt '01. The Anteaters had five players on the 13-man roster.

Souvenir Program
UCI's First Basketball Game

UC Irvine vs. **UC Riverside**

DECEMBER 1, 1965   CAMPUS HALL   TWENTY-FIVE CENTS

▼ *Frosh basketball team, November 1965.*

▼ *Varsity basketball Coach Dan Rogers (far right) with varsity players, from left, Dale Finney, Mark Nelson and Eldon McBride, November 1965.*

▲ *From the start, basketball is a*
▶ *major sport at UCI.*

Another inaugural sport—basketball—raised high hopes on December 1, 1965, when Aldrich held a ceremonial tipoff at center court of Campus Hall versus UC Riverside Chancellor Ivan Hinderaker. A full arena of spectators followed the cheerleaders in chants of "Zot!" while Coach Dan Rogers' varsity team, featuring 12 transfer students, won 85–71. The team went on to finish its first season with a 15–11 record.

The freshman team held its own that first year as well, losing only three games. "We were all naive in that we believed that we were going to be the best," alumnus Brande said. "We actually thought we were going to beat UCLA. Playing against this UCLA freshman player named Lew Alcindor [later Kareem Abdul-Jabbar] at Pauley Pavilion was the highlight of my athletic life." UC Irvine lost that game, he said, but it didn't matter.

Anteater athletic teams garnered 13 national championships during UCI's first decade, with men's swimming and diving bringing home that first NCAA championship in 1969. Women's sports were slower to find their footing. The first conference championship in women's sports was snared by the cross-

▶ *UCI swimming team defeated 81 other schools to win the NCAA College Division national championship in 1969 in Springfield, Massachusetts. Mike Martin, sophomore, won the 200-, 500- and 1,650-meter free-style events and had the fastest legs on the winning Anteater 400- and 800-free relay teams. Shown from left at UCI pool, Edward Newland, assistant coach, Al Irwin, coach, Tim Cooper, Mike Martin, Steve Farmer, Bob Drake, and Rich Eason.*

> "Every day I appreciated walking the campus with pride that I was among people who would catapult themselves to something special."
>
> —**Scott Brooks '87**
> UCI BASKETBALL POINT GUARD, 1985–1987;
> SPONSOR OF THE ANNUAL SCOTT BROOKS
> GOLF TOURNAMENT FUNDING UCI ATHLETIC
> SCHOLARSHIPS; AND CURRENT COACH OF NBA
> DIVISION TITLE-WINNING OKLAHOMA THUNDER

▶ *Dan Guerrero, fourth from left, Ralph Cicerone, second from left, and guests break ground on the baseball field.*

◀ *Anteater basketball phenom Kevin Magee and Bill Mulligan show great chemistry as player and coach.*

▶ *Linda Dempsey, the nation's first female athletic director of a Division I program.*

country team in 1983–1984. But UCI made history when Linda Dempsey—a volleyball, tennis and swimming coach—was named athletic director in 1978, becoming the nation's first woman to direct a Division I program.

The fledgling Anteater teams were moved up to NCAA Division I on July 1, 1977. In the early 1980s, men's basketball drew sellout crowds eager to see star player Kevin Magee, who had accompanied Coach Bill Mulligan to UC Irvine from nearby Saddleback College. Magee became a two-time first-team All-American, and UC Irvine earned a slot in the prestigious National Invitational Tournament in 1982. The 1986 team made its mark by doing the once unthinkable: upsetting UCLA. Slated to meet their neighbors at Pauley Pavilion in the NIT's first round, UC Irvine students lined up for several days before the game to purchase tickets and then braved a soggy March storm to trek to Westwood and witness the 80–74 victory. "The first time Orange County took us seriously was when we beat UCLA in basketball," Peltason told UC Irvine historian Spencer C. Olin many years later.

In 1987, the university and Orange County residents celebrated the opening of the Bren Events Center, which gave the basketball team a home court befitting a champion. While the students had long nursed an inferiority complex linked to the lack of a football team, the basketball team's success and the opening of the Bren Center seemed to finally put pigskin fever to rest. "It's not a gym; it's a real arena!" Mulligan exclaimed.

THE FIRST CUT IS THE DEEPEST

Spring 1992 brought budget and program cuts to athletics, but new athletic director Dan Guerrero was determined to strengthen some ailing programs, recruit top athletes and re-energize the fan base. He staged pizza and fudge giveaways and organized lively halftime entertainment.

► *The women's water polo team wins its fourth consecutive Big West Tournament Championship in 2012 and goes on to finish fourth at the NCAA Championship.*

► *UCI five-time All-American Elisabeth "Buffy" Rabbitt '91, who helped cross country finish fourth in the 1990 NCAA championship, the highest finish in team history up to that point.*

▼ *In 1997, Women's Soccer reaches a second straight Big West Tournament final, ultimately winning its first championship title.*

▼ *Kristina Smith, women's tennis player in 2010, comes from a long line of Anteaters. Her mother is an outstanding tennis player from the 1980s and her grandmother is also an alumna.*

▼ Gabby Pierandozzi, who
plays defense for UCI's
women's water polo team,
looks to pass the ball
during practice, 2014.

Once ignored, women's teams began achieving some success in the
1990s, and the women's soccer team of 1995–1996 was ranked in the nation's
top 25 Division I squads. The 1994–1995 women's basketball team won the
Big West Conference and the women's cross country teams won conference
titles five times that decade. By 2013, longtime women's
cross-country coach Vince O'Boyle had been named
conference Coach of the Year 20 times.

By the time the university reached its 35th
anniversary, the athletes had won the student body's
admiration. During the 1998–1999 school year, students
voted for a $33-per-quarter fee to support athletic
programs. Three additional women's sports were also
added, and funds were allocated to club sports, the pep
band and the pep squad.

And, despite naysayers who said it couldn't be done,
baseball was reinstated. The new team's first game was
held before 3,000 enthusiastic fans on January 25, 2002,
at the newly developed Anteater Ballpark. UC Irvine
qualified for postseason play seven times between 2004
and 2011 and appeared in the College World Series in
2007 and 2014. For a few weeks in the spring of 2009,
both the baseball and men's volleyball teams were
ranked first in the nation. The volleyball team won
the NCAA title that year, the start of a glorious era in
which it won four titles in seven years. "When that fee
referendum passed, it was the students realizing that
recognition of the athletic programs is directly related to
the value of your degree," Brande said. "When you talk to

◀ *Aaron Wright (No. 32) sinks a basket with John Ryan (No. 25) looking on in the 2014 Anteater win over UC Davis that clinched the league championship for UCI.*

people in the community, they talk about this or that championship. They don't talk about the chemistry professors, even though we have the best chemistry professors in the world."

Today, with programs that turn out not only fine athletes but accomplished students, 'Eater Nation stands tall. In seven of the past eight years, the university has ranked in the top five of the Division I-AAA Athletics Directors Association standings, a poll developed by the National Association of Collegiate Directors of Athletics and *USA Today* to rank Division I schools that don't sponsor football. UC Irvine now sponsors nine men's and nine women's teams and has, over the past half-century, earned 28 national titles, while individual students have won 64 national titles and 500 All-American honors.

▲ *The 2008 Men's Soccer team finishes the season with its first Big West Tournament title and NCAA berth, advancing to the Sweet Sixteen and entering the rankings for the first time ever, reaching as high as No. 7.*

▼ *Members of the 2012 men's volleyball NCAA Championship team. Signing T-shirts for appreciative Anteater fans.*

Current Athletic Teams and Founding Years

Men's

Basketball, 1965–1966
Golf, 1965–1966
Tennis, 1965–1966
Water polo, 1965–1966
Baseball, 1968–1969*
Cross country, 1971–1972
Track and field, 1971–1972
Volleyball, 1975–1976
Soccer, 1984–1985

Women's

Volleyball, 1967–1968
Tennis, 1973–1974
Basketball, 1974–1975
Track and field, 1976–1977
Cross country, 1979–1980
Soccer, 1984–1985
Golf, 2000–2001
Indoor track, 2000–2001
Water polo, 2000–2001

* The baseball program was disbanded in 1993 and reinstated in 2002.

▼ *Martial arts at the ARC.*　　▶ *A view from the shire, Middle Earth undergraduate housing complex.*

The Hobbit AND PLACES TO CALL HOME

In 1991, a new Anteater costume debuted. It was not well received. It was brown and pudgy and had gentle eyes; a decidedly nonthreatening creature that would not inspire fear in the hearts of athletic opponents. But students in the 1990s were concerned with weightier matters. The universitywide budget woes of the early 1990s were a drag on a campus trying to grow. The editor of the 1995 yearbook, Tracey Tardiff, summed up the sentiment: "In these changing times, as everyone becomes increasingly individualistic, the disparity between the needs and wants of the students, faculty, and administration is growing larger every day."

About 70 percent of students still commuted to campus, but that was about to change. An especially large freshman class in 1996 strained campus housing. The yearbook writers noted: "It's nice to know we're attending a university in demand."

A second on-campus housing unit for students had opened in 1976. The students named it Middle Earth after J.R.R. Tolkien's *The Hobbit*. The Campus Village apartment complex and the Arroyo Vista community of themed houses—biology, careers in teaching, Chicano/Latino studies—provided off-campus housing to students who still wanted to walk to classes. But the most significant explosion of campus housing occurred in more recent years with the development of the East Campus area, framed by Campus Drive, East Peltason Drive and Anteater Drive. The complexes include Verano Place, Palo Verde, Vista del Campo and Camino del Sol housing units, several of which won their builders awards for energy efficiency and amenities that include game rooms, conference rooms and hot tubs.

▼ *Students try out the climbing wall and other amenities at the Anteater Recreation Center's all-night Welcome Week event.*

The heart of East Campus, however, is the Anteater Recreation Center—known as the ARC. Opening in 2000 with support from additional student fees, the ARC marked a pinnacle in providing students with a hangout that didn't involve getting in a car and hitting the freeway. The popular recreation center features outdoor fields, weight rooms, an indoor jogging track, a pool, sports courts, a rock climbing wall,

◀ *ARC's suspended indoor track accommodates a runner, far away from other bustling activity below.*

a fitness lab and more. Ten years after its debut, an expansion resulted in a wellness lab and a test kitchen. The ARC now contains more than 30 tons of free weights, thus ensuring that any Anteater can be a buff Anteater.

Today, freshmen are guaranteed two years of housing, and 80 percent of freshmen live on campus. Just over half of all students either live on campus or are within walking distance. And they're not the only ones who can stroll to class. UC Irvine distinguished itself from most US campuses when University Hills, on the south edge of campus, was developed to house faculty and staff. The community had its origins in discussions between Aldrich and university planner Ray L. Watson, who championed a "town and gown" partnership between the campus and the city of Irvine. Watson envisioned the university as the heart of the city and hoped that businesses, housing developments, restaurants and shops would radiate out from the campus after its founding.

"Aldrich always talked about a residential university for faculty, staff and students," recalled professor William Parker, who collaborated with professor James McGaugh to lobby for University Hills. By the early 1980s, housing prices in Orange County were soaring and posed a problem when it came to convincing potential new faculty members to accept positions at UCI. University Hills was based on the idea that housing prices could only appreciate within a preset range, thus keeping the homes affordable.

The complex was developed on the 510 acres that the regents had wisely purchased back in the 1960s for future needs. The first homes were completed in 1986, and over the next several years, more homes were built along with community swimming pools, playgrounds and preschools. For many instructors and staff, the commute to class or work is about three minutes on bike or 10 minutes by foot. "University Hills has worked tremendously in recruiting faculty," Parker said. "We've been able to offer affordable housing to just about everybody we've recruited. I don't think any place in the country has done what we've done."

▼ *Anteater Express eliminates need for students to drive to class while reducing traffic congestion and emissions.*

▼ *The Anteater Spirit Quad and Pep Band motivate fans, athletes.*

DANCE AND OTHER REVOLUTIONS

The turn of the century dawned on a UC Irvine campus that had survived growing pains in the 1980s and 1990s and blossomed into one of the most highly respected public universities in the nation. Undergraduate enrollment topped 22,000 by 2005. So many students now traversed the campus that stricter rules were written to limit skateboarders' and bicyclists' use of Ring Mall. To ease parking and transportation woes, free shuttle buses carried students to and from housing communities. Rental cars called Zipcars and rental bikes known as ZotWheels were purchased. The need to reduce automobile traffic blended well with the university's growing reputation as one of the greenest schools in the country.

Some students gave up car ownership out of financial necessity. The Great Recession battered the California economy and led to soaring UC fees throughout the first dozen years of the new century. In the fall of 2009, hundreds of faculty, staff and students walked out of classes to protest a 32 percent tuition hike. Fee protests were a routine part of student life at UC Irvine and other UC campuses. The 85,000 people who now called themselves UC Irvine alumni were grateful they had attended the school when both fees and admission criteria were considerably lower.

▼ *From Oingo Boingo to comedienne Gilda Radner, countless big-name bands and celebrities have provided entertainment in the park over the years.*

By the early 2000s, UC Irvine's increasingly selective admissions process was something to be celebrated. Many academic programs had emerged as the best in their fields, and UCI students had created a reputation for themselves as smart, creative, tech-savvy and entrepreneurial. The word "apathy" is rarely heard on campus these days.

UC Irvine brings more students to UC Student Lobby Conferences than any other campus, said Justin Chung, the 2013 president of Associated Graduate Students. Instead of attempting to copy traditions begun a century ago at other US universities, UCI students focus on activities unique to them, such as the video game development club, a student-run organization in which students design games and pitch their ideas to members for feedback. "This group exists because of students, not because some professor cared about doing this," Chung said. "Students make their own fun here. You make your own future here. It is a new university."

Music and dancing, in particular, have provided a core identity to a student body that was for so many years in search of one. The university's dance crew phenomenon had modest beginnings in 1996 when the Lambda Theta Delta fraternity held a small hip-hop dance competition. The event, called Vibe, exploded in popularity. Hundreds of students converged on the Bren Events Center on November 15, 2005, to watch the UC Irvine chapter of Hip Hop Congress perform. Noted one student: "Who else can say they root for dance crews instead of a football team? That's because no one else has moves like we do."

By 2006, the event had begun to attract hip-hop enthusiasts from around Southern California. One UC Irvine group, Kaba Modern, won second place at the 2007 World Hip Hop Dance Championship. Other music-related events also draw enthusiastic support from students, including Reggaefest, held in Aldrich Park at the end of each academic year, and Soulstice, a talent competition founded in 2012 featuring dance, a capella, band, solo and duet performances as well as skits.

Students have found other unique ways to elevate the UC Irvine name. Welcome Week 2010 featured an attempt to set a world record for the largest dodgeball game ever. Hundreds of students converged on the Bren Events Center to compete but the start of the match was postponed when officials noted there were too few players to set the record. Tweets, texts and Facebook posts flooded all avenues of student communication, and 1,745 competitors

◄ *Reggae Fest in Aldrich Park gives students a break from studying from finals, June 2013.*

▶ *Dodgeball record seesaws for three years before UCI last claims it in 2012 with 6,084 participants.*

▼ *Recent Welcome Week tradition includes a Guinness World Record-breaking event. In 2013, it's a water blaster fight.*

were soon on hand to break the world record. Five months later, the title was lost to the University of Alberta, Canada, so a revenge match was held in 2011 on the ARC fields.

"Referees were enlisted to enforce the rules and shrink the game field, but everyone knew that having fun came first," wrote the yearbook editors. A new record was set, but the pesky Canadians wrenched it back, and in 2012, 6,084 UCI students chanting "Hit me with your best 'Zot!'" once again gathered to set the record straight. In September 2013, the students mixed things up a bit, choosing instead to attempt the world's largest water-blaster battle. The 3,875 watergun-toting combatants easily took the record from the previous holder, the residents of Valladolid, Spain, and in 2014 4,200 participants set a record for the world's largest pillow fight.

After almost 50 years, some traditions continue and new ones form.

"This is the dynamic that we pursue here," said Parham, "educating the whole student. It's about the classroom, yes, but it's also about cocurricular activities, learning how to forge your own path, make your education and your future what you want it to be. We nurture leaders. There's no place quite like it."

▲ UCI is home to the West
◄ Coast's first major hip-hop
competition, VIBE, created in
2005 by Asian American
fraternity Lambda Theta Delta.

Anteaters celebrate with men's basketball team members after winning the league championship in March 2014.

▲ Members of UCI's track teams pause during a spring meet in 2014.

▲ Paige Bushnell (No. 6) takes off after a smooth baton pass from teammate Melanie Speech during relay.

◄◄ Pole vaulter Ariel Cheng and hurdler Kaulyn Lee-McNeill.

chapter 5

campus as catalyst

Sometimes the best ideas come from the most unexpected places. For J. Stuart Nelson, it was a TV baseball broadcast.

The medical director of UC Irvine's Beckman Laser Institute and Medical Clinic was puzzling over how to laser away unwanted blood vessels that result in disfiguring port-wine stain birthmarks while leaving the outer skin undamaged. He watched baseball trainers spray coolant over aching ankles hit by foul tips, and noticed that the substance evaporated instantly without harming the skin. That was his "aha!" moment.

◀ *Watson Bridge, named after Irvine city planner and Irvine Company President Ray L. Watson, connects UCI to the city.*

◀ *Gateway Plaza is a bustling crossroads for UCI students.*

5

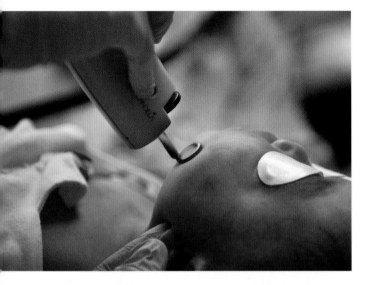

▼ *A prime example of UCI ingenuity, the Beckman Laser Institute and Medical Clinic's Dynamic Cooling Device revolutionized laser surgery.*

After much tinkering, Nelson and his colleagues developed the Dynamic Cooling Device, which had a similar effect, but also eliminated the unsightly birthmarks. It debuted in 1998, and by 2014 tens of thousands of the specialized lasers had been sold worldwide.

It's the same kind of ingenuity the university's researchers use to solve once elusive problems. It's the brand of inventiveness that has brought three Nobel Prizes, numerous other honors and international recognition to UC Irvine during its first 50 years. And it's the kind of breakthrough that faculty build upon to produce yet more discoveries. The laser device patent has generated more than $40 million in royalties, much of it plowed back into the institute and other corners of the campus for additional research.

UC Irvine biotech researchers have launched dozens of start-up companies to conduct the rigorous clinical trials that major pharmaceutical companies are often loath to undertake. Biophysics professor George Chandy created Airmid Inc. in 2000 to develop autoimmune drugs from shrub and sea anemone compounds. Bioengineer Joyce Keyak, who cofounded Bone-Rad Therapeutics, Inc., was named to *Image*'s "25 Most Influential in Radiology" roster for her work creating radioactive bone cement that targets cancerous tumors in the bone without damaging surrounding healthy tissue.

▲ *From left, Jeff Greenberg, Stephen Jenks and Sung-Jin Kim, inventors of the HIPerwall at UCI's Calit2. They have installed hundreds of the display systems worldwide.*

▶ *Exhibits at the pioneering Beall Center for Art + Technology explore new relationships between the arts, sciences and engineering.*

▲ Donald R. Beall and his wife, Joan, receive a star on UCI's Claire Trevor School of the Arts Walk of Fame for their longtime support of the arts, March 10, 2014. They also fund entreprenurial programs.

> "I'm inspired by UCI's ongoing commitment to translating the extraordinary talents of its faculty and students in ways that ensure a vibrant ecosystem of innovation."
>
> —Richard Sudek
> EXECUTIVE DIRECTOR OF THE
> UCI INSTITUTE FOR INNOVATION

The numbers help tell the story: The university's research has yielded more than 60 spin-off companies, 901 inventions, 334 active patents and 113 active license or option agreements.

In February 2014, the university created the Institute for Innovation, a campuswide entity to help leverage more research into entrepreneurial endeavors that benefit society. Made possible by a $5 million endowment from the Beall Family Foundation, it will be an epicenter of innovation for the county, bringing together a community of faculty, students, entrepreneurs and industry to turn research breakthroughs into real-world applications, said Howard Gillman, appointed UCI's provost and executive vice chancellor in June 2013 and chancellor in September 2014.

"We already make tremendous contributions to the economic vitality of the region and to transforming our discoveries into innovations that address important social needs," Gillman said. "But there is more that we can do, and the new Institute for Innovation will ensure that we reach our full potential by working closely with our community partners."

Perhaps the university's most important community partner is the very city with which it developed. "Irvine has grown alongside us and has had tremendous accomplishments, just as we have had," Gillman said. "We've shared those accomplishments together."

One endeavor neither the city nor the campus could have achieved on their own was the building of the Irvine Barclay Theatre. Irvine and UCI

Good at Acting Up

Jon Lovitz may be the most recognizable UCI alumnus to make his career in arts and entertainment. He parlayed his theater degree into a gig with The Groundlings comedy troupe, and then starred as a cast member on *Saturday Night Live* in the late 1980s where his "Master Thespian" character imitated a former professor. Lovitz went on to a long film and television career, including *Mom and Dad Save the World* and *City Stickers II: The Legend of Curly's Gold*. He now owns the Jon Lovitz Comedy Club & Podcast Theatre in Universal City, California.

▲ *Jon Lovitz '79.*

Windell Middlebrooks, who earned an MFA in acting in 2004, appeared in dozens of shows. He had recurring characters in *It's Always Sunny in Philadelphia* and *Body of Proof*. But he may have been most familiar to viewers as a Miller High Life beer delivery driver, advertisements that jumpstarted his career in 2008. He died suddenly in 2015.

Some alumni have excelled behind the camera, including Joseph McGinty "McG" Nichol, director of the *Charlie's Angels* films and *Terminator Salvation*. The psychology major's executive producer credits include TV show *The O.C.*, which drew on his memories of growing up in Newport Beach. His nickname, McG, isn't some entertainment-industry affectation. His uncle and grandfather were also named Joe, so his mother called him McG to avoid confusion, and it stuck.

had each dreamed of a community theater, but funding was elusive. Then, in the late 1980s, UC Irvine offered 2.3 acres of prime real estate at the university's entrance in return for use of the theater one-third of the time.

▲ *Windell Middlebrooks MFA '04.*

As the cost grew, then-Chancellor Jack W. Peltason agreed to put $1.8 million toward the project if the city and nonprofit theater operating company came up with the rest. Richard and Marjorie Barclay, real estate developers who also supported the medical school, pledged an additional $1 million, followed by $750,000 more from George and Arlene Cheng, longtime supporters of the arts and UC Irvine. The 750-seat Irvine Barclay Theatre opened on September 30, 1990, and continues to host a dazzling array of multicultural acts and top international performers.

"That was very important symbolically," said Larry Agran, a longtime Irvine resident and former mayor. Agran applauds the city-university partnership that built the theater as "an extraordinary success, and with the theater right there on the campus, that helps cement our relationship."

In another collaboration, Agran sought chemistry professor F. Sherwood Rowland's expertise in climate science before developing the 1989 city law that made it illegal to buy, sell or use products containing harmful chlorofluorocarbons. Many other local governments followed suit and passed similar measures before the nation began a broader phaseout of the chemicals.

Taking Shakespeare out of the classroom to a venue under the stars, UCI's New Swan Theatre makes its debut in summer 2012. The two-tiered facility seats 125 people, providing an intimate setting guaranteed to please Bard-lovers. "Shakespeare festivals around the country are beloved gathering places for people with a passion for great literature, powerful productions and exciting performances," says UCI drama professor Eli Simon, who launched the project. "The impact on the campus and community is profound and positive."

Bridging the Gap

A pedestrian bridge linking UC Irvine with the community was Ray L. Watson's grand idea in the mid-1960s, but it took a long time to reach fruition. The Irvine Company's chief architect and planner helped William Pereira with his master plan. Watson worried that the city and university might drift apart, and he wanted the bridge to be a symbolic bond. But he couldn't get it built at first.

On October 26, 1970, an untimely firebomb tossed at the nearby Bank of America branch stirred concerns about student radicals, though no student was ever tied to the event. The bridge plans were shelved. Watson patiently knit together town and gown in the company's planning and, later, as Irvine Company president. Still, no bridge.

He finally saw it built in 1985. Twenty years later—more than four decades after he began his quest—Watson received some overdue recognition. One fall afternoon in 2005, 200 invited guests stood by the symbolic span and formally named it for the man who had fought so long to build it. Irvine Company Chairman Donald Bren told the crowd: "We considered Ray to be the keeper of the flame for the original ideas and concepts behind Irvine's master plan."

▲ *Ray L. Watson (1926–2012) helps create an economically viable community with a university—UCI—at its center.*

▲ *The September 1966 issue of* Orange County Illustrated *showcases a painting of UCI, c. 1966, by renowned California watercolorist Rex Brandt. The* Orange County Progress Report *features an aerial shot of campus from the early 1960s.*

The Montreal Protocol at about the same time called for a ban on the worldwide production of most CFCs by the year 2000.

The parallels between town and gown are numerous. Irvine didn't really emerge until after the university burst into existence, formally incorporating on December 28, 1971, with a little more than 14,000 residents. Like the university, Irvine grew swiftly through much of the 1970s and 1980s—and is still one of the fastest-growing cities in the United States. It now has 230,000-plus residents, while the campus has more than 30,000 students. Like the university, the city grew up with a sense that it was unique, destined for greatness. Irvine takes special pride in its 1988 Open Space Initiative, which protects more than 16,000 acres of parks and wildlands in perpetuity. Both the university and the city were master-planned by architect William Pereira, and both share his love of greenbelts. Both also are leaders in environmental planning, recycled water and the construction of "green" buildings. The university and the city were made for each other—literally.

▲ *Signage for University Center in its early days points individuals to the local US Post Office branch, Bank of America, a drycleaners and a popular beer garden restaurant.*

▼ *UCI's San Joaquin Marsh Reserve, a UC Natural Reserve*
▲ *System, doubles as a living laboratory for biological sciences students and a nature attraction for the community.*

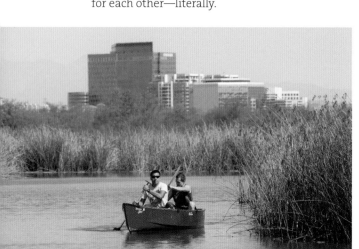

Steven Choi, elected mayor in 2012, sees the campus as a major partner in bringing even more high-tech industries to the city. He hopes to see the technological might of the city and UC Irvine someday rival that of Northern California's Silicon Valley.

"We have the space to make it," Choi said. "Our vision and their vision are very much the same. Another Google and another Facebook may come out of our efforts in the future here. We have our own technology cluster that's only going to grow." He added that Irvine is geographically "uniquely situated" between Los Angeles and San Diego, and that the city's reputation for safety and excellent schools, combined with UC Irvine's brainpower and research facilities, increasingly make it a great place for technologically minded companies and their employees to settle. "We need to continue to build on that and work together," Choi said.

Added Gillman: "We are building systematic bridges ... to allow us to develop, arm in arm, with a very talented and still young and ambitious community. The faculty has drawn inspiration from the community, and vice versa."

> *"I did not invent the Internet—which some people joke about. But I was the primary architect of the current version, HTTP/1.1."*
>
> —Paul Mockapetris, PhD '82

Clicking Across the Frontiers of Science

If Paul Mockapetris didn't exactly invent the Internet, he sure played a major role in its creation—enough to get him inducted into the Internet Hall of Fame. Shortly after earning his computer science doctorate from UCI in 1982, Mockapetris proposed opening up the academics-only ARPANET (predecessor to the Internet) to everyone. He created the Domain Name System— essentially, the Internet's phone book. It became a key part of the Internet as it hit everyone's computers in the 1990s. He now works for Nominum, a network security firm, where he devises ways to defeat viruses, Trojan horses and other malicious mischief.

Following in his footsteps was Roy T. Fielding. He already had made an impact on the Internet's development, working with Timothy Berners-Lee on major improvements to the World Wide Web's infrastructure in the mid-1990s. He honed his skills and earned a doctorate at UC Irvine, was named one of 100 top young innovators by *MIT Technology Review* in 1999, and is now principal scientist at Adobe Systems in San Jose.

Of course, not every UC Irvine-trained scientist deals with zeros and ones. Cynthia Woo, now an assistant project scientist at UCI, worked with fellow neurobiologist Michael Leon on a study that showed autistic boys improved their social skills significantly after exercises in which they smelled lavender, lemon, apple and vanilla, and listened to classical music. Kathy L. Olsen followed up her neuroscience doctorate with a long career that included serving as senior scientist at NASA and senior adviser at the National Science Foundation, as well as founding ScienceWorks, which helps academic institutions craft science programs. Robin Cotton's doctorate in molecular biology and biochemistry led to a career testifying about DNA evidence in hundreds of criminal cases across the country. And Tina Nova used her biology degree to found Genoptix, a molecular diagnostics company. Nova was ranked among the top 10 women in biotech by the industry newsletter *FierceBiotech*.

▶ *Roy T. Fielding PhD '00, a principal author of the now-familiar HTTP application protocol that guides the flow of information over the Internet.*

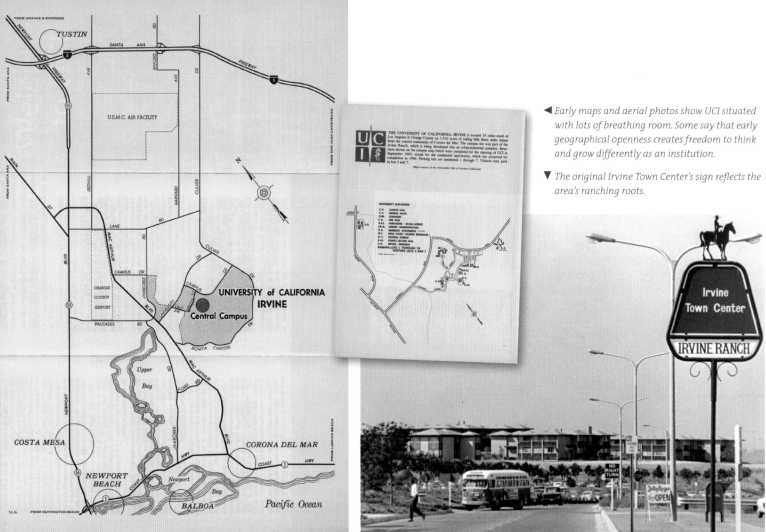

ROOM TO GROW

A key ingredient in UC Irvine's growth and bright future lies all around the campus: land. Many universities are essentially built out, unable to expand without aggravating their neighbors. Irvine's campus would be facing the same dilemma today if the university had settled for the 650 acres first offered by the Irvine Company, back in 1959. Negotiations eventually resulted in 1,000 acres.

And it didn't end there. After more discussions, the Irvine Company sold at a discount an additional 510 acres, intended originally for normal university activities. By the time the campus got around to considering what to do with that land, the times had changed. What UC Irvine really needed in the mid-1980s was something new: University Research Park, a place where the university and private businesses could join in mutually beneficial projects.

This was the new concept of "research to market." The university does the research, and businesses use that work to do what they do best—make better products. UC Irvine collects millions of dollars in payments, and that money goes to the Bren Fellows Program of endowed chairs.

► *Ophthalmologist Marjan Farid operates on a patient with macular degeneration, implanting a miniature telescope designed to restore lost vision, 2011.*

▼ *A preemie at UC Irvine Douglas Hospital's neonatal intensive care unit receives quality cuddle time.*

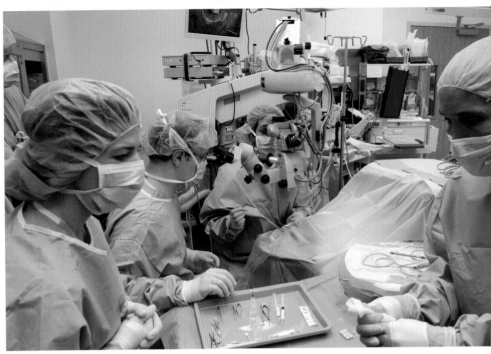

"On my first visit to UCI 30 years ago, I found the campus to be interactive, collaborative, energetic and supportive. It's still that way today."

—Frances Leslie
DEAN OF GRADUATE EDUCATION
AND PROFESSOR OF PHARMACOLOGY

In 2005, the research park added its biggest piece yet: the computer chipmaker Broadcom, whose founders have been kind to UC Irvine in other ways. Henry Samueli and Henry Nicholas jointly gave $3 million to create UCI's Center for Pervasive Communications and Computing. Samueli gave an additional $20 million to the university's School of Engineering. After the 2005 deal, University Research Park packed in about 40 companies.

"Knowledge-based industries, biomedical instrumentation, semiconductor companies, and video games are now at UCI," former Chancellor Ralph J. Cicerone said after he left to head the National Academy of Sciences in 2005. "That's all clustering around the campus. They are all looking for students to hire, and researchers to interact with. Some people questioned whether we could be a great research university. I think it's been handled pretty well."

Thirteen miles away in Orange sits UC Irvine Douglas Hospital, completed in 2009 as part of UCI Medical Center. The seven-story project gave the university a modern facility for training physicians, conducting research and treating patients. The building was named after a $21 million posthumous gift from real estate developer M.A. Douglas.

The hospital has come a long way since UC Irvine acquired it from the county in the 1970s. It has grown steadily in size and reputation, ranked among the nation's best hospitals for 14 straight years, as of 2014, by *U.S. News & World Report*. The hospital is often first with new treatments and groundbreaking research, including the first heart transplant in Orange County, the first insulin pump implant on the West Coast in a diabetes patient and numerous breakthroughs in cancer research.

◀ *Daniel Poneman, US Department of Energy deputy secretary (2009–2014), talks with students and faculty in the Henry Samueli School of Engineering about alternative energy, February 2014. He also announces UCI is part of an Orange County-based team in the 2015 Solar Decathlon, which pits college and university teams in competition to build the best sustainable home.*

▶ *Students cross Watson Bridge over Campus Drive to University Center (formerly Irvine Town Center), where restaurants supplement campus eateries and a movie theater offers escape from studying.*

▼ *Scientists study climate change, water supply and visitor use of delicate desert parkland at the Steele/Burnand Anza-Borrego Desert Research Center. A historic clubhouse is now a long-sought UCI field research center thanks to a gift from Audrey Steele Burnand.*

▼ *The largest single individual donation to UCI comes from Paul Merage, creator of Hot Pockets and the signature sleeve that allows the turnovers to emerge crispy from the microwave. The School of Business carries his name.*

THE PERSONAL TOUCH

Billionaire Paul Merage was looking for a place to put his money to good use, training the next generation of entrepreneurs. He could have chosen UC Berkeley, his alma mater. Instead, he selected UC Irvine, giving the university $30 million, the largest single gift the campus had ever received. UCI renamed its business school in Merage's honor.

"It's a young, dynamic business school," said Merage, who created the microwavable snack Hot Pockets and built it into a billion-dollar business with his brother David. "It's more apt to change with the times than older, more established business schools. The rapid pace of change today means the world 10 years from now is going to be very different."

Only 16 when he arrived in America from Iran, Merage and his brother struggled for years, taking out a second and then a third mortgage on his house, borrowing money from their parents, enduring damage from a factory fire and the 1994 Northridge earthquake. But the two persevered, growing the business into one of the nation's largest privately held food-processing companies. "We had to think outside of the box to find the right ingredients and processes that would make a Hot Pocket emerge from the microwave crispy instead of soggy. A professional baker wouldn't have even tried to do that," Merage said. He believes UC Irvine can nurture and inspire entrepreneurs with the same inventiveness and resilience so that they can create their own success stories.

What Merage wanted most from UCI's business school was personalization, giving students the attention and guidance they need to become successful business leaders. He found then-Chancellor Cicerone and former business school Dean Andrew Policano very much in tune with his ideas. "UC Irvine is a special institution with a great capacity to continue to excel and grow," he said. "It can help shape the future of our nation and the world for generations to come."

> "Any undergraduate who has an idea can see it become a reality. Entrepreneurship is a wonderful way to think of your own future."
>
> —Sharon Salinger
> THEN-DEAN OF UNDERGRADUATE EDUCATION ON THE OPENING OF THE BLACKSTONE LAUNCHPAD

▲ *Chancellor Michael V. Drake leads cyclists on a tour of Irvine, combining fun, fitness and fundraising for UC scholarships.*

▼ *Still in growth mode, the Paul Merage School of Business completes a new building in 2014 that features education and meeting spaces for three to 300, a coffeehouse and a food court.*

Pedaling for fun and dollars

One day in early 2014, then-Chancellor Michael V. Drake slapped a helmet on his head and took off on a 25-mile bike ride with 50 campus supporters in tow—an event called the "Tour of Irvine." Elsewhere, Rameen Talesh, assistant vice chancellor for student life and leadership, broke into song in front of the Student Center. And Dean William Maurer and School of Social Sciences staff strolled around campus dressed as *Star Trek* characters. "This makes me want to be accepted into UC Irvine even more!" posted an applicant for the fall.

Fundraising is both fun and serious business at the university. Pledge campaigns like this one organized by the University of California raise money for scholarships. Drake's bike ride generated more than $20,000, by far the largest yield of all the pledge efforts. UC Irvine had at least twice the number of participants than the closest competing UC campus.

"We are interested in nontraditional ways of fundraising," Drake said. One was crowdfunding, spreading the word through social media to get creative ideas for pledges and inspire participation. "We're particularly hoping to reach young people," Drake said, "so they can feel they are a part of it."

The campus's $1 billion "Shaping the Future" initiative began in 2005 and is designed to fund research, endowed chairs, scholarships and other campus projects.

Private money from philanthropists and grassroots efforts fueled much of UC Irvine's growth in its first 50 years, and it will play an even bigger role in the future. In addition to erecting more buildings and hiring more faculty and staff, the hundreds of millions of dollars raised by the Shaping the Future campaign has helped the campus create or revamp programs in pharmaceutical sciences, nursing, public health, law, education, gaming theory and business.

Finding greatness

Greatness doesn't always come in million-dollar pledges, endowed chairs and Nobel Prizes. Sometimes, it's a law student researching a pro bono case for an indigent client, or a nursing student staffing a community clinic, or a professor delivering a public lecture about his or her latest research. A university's soul is in the details, the little things that faculty, students and staff do to make Irvine and Orange County better places to live. It began

▲ The annual All-University Alumni picnic, in spring 1966, attracts a good turnout of families in a homespun event that combines picnicking, games and contests in a park not yet filled out with shade trees.

▶ In 2013, the campus opens a sparkling new home—the Newkirk Alumni Center. Martha Newkirk '72, MA '76, PhD '81, and her husband James (honorary '12) provide funding to start construction.

NEWKIRK ALUMNI CENTER

▲ *High school tours of the campus began as soon as the doors opened in 1965.*

with the founding faculty and the first students and continues to drive much of what UC Irvine does today.

"In addition to making contributions to basic science and fundamental inquiry, our very best people want to know that they can change the world with their ideas," Gillman said. "They want to know they're at an institution that will help them accomplish their vision. That's what our students want as well."

There are many examples around UC Irvine, whether it's Elizabeth Loftus, Distinguished Professor of Social Ecology and Law whose work in understanding human memory has cast doubt on the reliability of eye-witness testimony in criminal cases; or Scott Samuelsen, engineering professor and director of the National Fuel Cell Research Center, developing fuel cells that run cars, buildings and other systems more efficiently; or physicians at UC Irvine Medical Center testing new treatments for cancer; or social science professors studying the effects of economic policy on the working class.

In teacher education, the Cal Teach program prepares dozens of students each year for the rigors of teaching math and science in the state's most disadvantaged schools. Participants get their degrees and teaching credentials in four years instead of the usual five. The program is funded by the university, with support from the Hubert H. Wakeham Fund and the

► *The School of Education trains the teachers of tomorrow and fosters much-needed research on learning under the leadership of Deborah Lowe Vandell, founding dean.*

A Diverse Body Politic

Ten-year-old Van Tran knew exactly two English words, "OK" and "Salem" (cigarettes), when his family fled communist forces in Vietnam. He grew up to earn a political science degree from UC Irvine and became a political kingmaker in Orange County's Little Saigon neighborhoods. He was the first Vietnamese American to serve in a state legislature, the California Assembly, and one of many UCI alumni to find electoral success in Orange County and beyond.

Another Little Saigon politician, alumna Janet Nguyen, became the first Asian American to serve on the Orange County Board of Supervisors in 2007, after one of the closest elections in the county's history. After a recount and a court battle, the political science major was declared the winner by only three votes.

William R. "Bill" Leonard, a graduate in history, held elective office for decades in the state Assembly, Senate and Board of Equalization. His "Leonard Law" was the nation's only legislation extending First Amendment rights to private college and university students.

Ami Bera, the son of immigrants from India, defeated longtime Republican stalwart Dan Lungren in 2012 for a seat in the US House of Representatives. Before entering politics, he became a doctor after earning a biology degree and an MD at UCI. José Solorio, the son of migrant farmworkers who earned a bachelor's degree in social ecology, served in the Assembly for six years.

Orange Mayor Teresa "Tita" Smith's California roots go back seven generations. The lifelong resident of Orange founded the Old Towne Preservation Association. She has served the city on commissions and city council since 1992. A member of UCI's inaugural class, she voted for the Anteater mascot and "Zot!" battle cry.

▲ *Janet Nguyen '00.*

◀◀ *Ami Bera '87.*
◀ *Teresa Smith '70.*

▲ *His Holiness the XIV Dalai Lama greets Chancellor Drake and UCI Dalai Lama Scholars Armaan Rowther, Doug Cheung, Jasmine Fang and Moran Cohen. The Dalai Lama was making his second appearance at UCI as part of the Living Peace Series presented by the university and Orange County's Center for Living Peace.*

National Math + Science Initiative. "With the rigorous courses in science, math and education, Cal Teach is sending truly remarkable young teachers into our local schools," Drake said. "This represents an important pipeline of education talent for our community, region and state."

Drake was a proponent of experiential learning—using community service and internships not just as a way to learn, but a way to help people. He preached an inclusiveness that creates a welcoming and nurturing atmosphere for faculty, staff and students—an environment in which leaders are born.

Looking forward, administrators at a still young and hungry UC Irvine know the best days lie ahead. "No university in the country established in the last 50 years has risen as far or as fast as we have," Gillman said. "Our faculty is among the very best in the country. We attract the best and brightest students, and we combine a remarkable record of student success with the mission of expanding access to higher education.

"Our success is an affirmation of the excellence and innovative spirit we have nurtured since Lyndon B. Johnson dedicated our grounds in 1964. Today, as we head into the next 50 years, we have the opportunity to cement our reputation as a globally preeminent institution in the eyes of the nation and the world."

"You're the Antidote to Cynicism"

"Hello, Anteaters!" President Barack Obama called out to UC Irvine's 2014 graduating class. He paused for cheers, and then added with a wide grin: "That is something I never thought I'd say."

The president proved to be a quick study in UC Irvine culture, executing a proper Anteater sign, under Chancellor Michael V. Drake's tutelage. Nearly 7,000 students earning undergraduate, graduate and professional degrees joined them in a spirited "Zot! Zot! Zot!" About 30,000 parents, friends and campus supporters watched from the stands at Angel Stadium of Anaheim— seats acquired with the hottest tickets in town.

What brought the president to UC Irvine's June 14, 2014, commencement? "I'm here for a simple reason," Obama said. "You asked." An onslaught of 10,000 postcards signed by students, faculty, staff and alumni, plus a student-produced video delivered to the White House at the conclusion of a well-

▼ *President Barack Obama, speaking at UCI commencement 2014 on a platform in the outfield at Angel Stadium of Anaheim, thanks students for inviting him and also thanks Angels' MVP center fielder Mike Trout for sharing his turf.*

"UCI is ahead of the curve. You are all ahead of the curve."

—**President Barack Obama**
SPEAKING TO THE 2014 GRADUATING CLASS

AB0614
$ 0.00
T226
$
AC 128X
H
ANG1820
A20MAY4

SECTION/AISLE ROW/BOX SEAT   ADMISSION
TERRACE   1   A-TYPE EAB0614
TERRACE
                    0.00   T226
UC IRVINE COMMENCEMENT   ETC CN 16800
FEATURED SPEAKER   AC500ANG
PRESIDENT BARACK OBAMA   H
JUNE 14 2014 10:30AM   0.00

0043788803767

ticketmaster

BUY TICKETS AT TICKETMASTER.COM

University of California, Irvine
49th Commencement

Saturday, June 14, 2014

FEATURED SPEAKER
BARACK OBAMA
PRESIDENT OF THE UNITED STATES

▲ *Nearly 30,000 graduates, their family members, alumni and friends fill the stadium to hear Obama's 25-minute speech. Ticket stubs and commencement programs quickly become collectors' items.*

organized six-month campaign encouraged him to attend commencement, which also marked the kickoff to the campus's 50th anniversary celebration.

"Some tried to guilt me into coming," Obama added, noting some clever postcard pleas. "I got one that said, 'I went to your first inauguration. Can you please come to my graduation?' Some tried bribery: 'I will support the Chicago Bulls.'"

In the video, 7-foot-6-inch Anteater basketball center Mamadou Ndiaye towers over a life-size cardboard cutout of Obama. "Mr. President, we should play ball together," he suggests, strategically playing to the president's love of basketball.

Hours before Obama arrived, a line snaked around the stadium. Students began arriving as early as 6 a.m. with their coveted four tickets per family in hand. The crowd watched UCI vocal groups Circle of Fifths and Vermillion Vocalists onstage, answered UCI trivia, and cheered audience Tweets and Instagram photos posted to the Jumbotron. In the massive student robing tent, graduating seniors flocked to dozens of "selfie" stations for pictures of themselves with Peter the Anteater and other iconic UCI backdrops.

Taking the stage shortly after noon, Obama paid tribute to UC Irvine's accomplishments and its unique character. "Keep in mind, you're not only the number-one university in

America younger than 50 years old," the president said, "you also hold the Guinness World Record for biggest water pistol fight." The crowd reacted with thunderous applause. Obama also acknowledged UC Irvine's baseball team playing that day in the College World Series.

His 30-minute speech soon zeroed in on climate change—appropriate for the university where F. Sherwood Rowland and Mario J. Molina's Nobel Prize-winning research proved that man-made chlorofluorocarbons were damaging the Earth's protective ozone layer. Obama lauded the campus for creating the first department of Earth system science in the nation, noting that a UCI glaciologist's findings about the irreversible retreat of the world's ice sheets had made recent headlines. The president commended the university for reducing its energy use by 20 percent seven years ahead of his 2020 challenge to colleges and universities. "UCI is ahead of the curve," Obama said.

James L. McGaugh, professor of neurobiology and behavior and founding faculty member, had watched President Lyndon B. Johnson dedicate the nascent campus in 1964. At 82, he was among the platform party that greeted Obama.

"Fifty years ago, at the dedication of this campus, there was a sense of excitement mixed with naiveté because we were all so young," McGaugh said. "There was an air of freedom because we were not confined or constrained and we were going to create a new university in our image.

"Today, with President Obama recognizing UC Irvine's contributions to research on the environment, and with us filling Angel Stadium with students and family for commencement, this no longer marks a beginning," he continued. "We are established and celebrating UCI's major achievements."

While President Johnson had emphasized the need for higher education in his dedication speech 50 years ago, Obama called for action on climate change, arguing that it is already a major threat, with increasingly harsh

▶ *UCI staff member Bill Reddel directs volunteers on the field at Angel Stadium. His task? Seat 8,000 giddy graduates in 30 minutes.*

▼ *The Big A along the 57 Freeway features Peter the Anteater for the first time in history.*

◀ *Chancellor Michael V. Drake bestows President Obama with the UCI Medal, the campus's highest honor.*

Marine One whisks the president away through a cloudless sky, June 14, 2014.

▲ *Students, who gather at 6 a.m. on commencement day, are still smiling brightly at noon following President Obama's keynote address and the turning of their tassels.*

▼ *Giving a historic "Zot!" cheer at commencement 2014 are, counterclockwise from upper left: Howard Gillman, (now) chancellor; Ralph Clayman, dean of the school of medicine; Jessica Pratt, graduate commencement speaker; Jennifer Rodriguez, undergraduate commencement speaker; and President Obama.*

droughts, fires, storms and floods. He stressed the need for a low-carbon, clean-energy economy.

Obama expressed confidence that the generation of students he called "the most educated, the most diverse, the most tolerant, the most politically independent and the most digitally fluent in our history" could get the job done noting that they are "on record as being the most optimistic about our future." He highlighted the inspirational strength of graduating students: Aaron Anderson, who joined the Army Special Forces after 9/11 and was nearly killed by a roadside bomb, graduating *summa cum laude*; Mohamad Abedi, who grew up in Lebanese refugee camps and now studies the human brain as a biomedical engineer; and Cinthia Flores, UC student regent, who earned a law degree to protect the rights of people like her mom, a seamstress and housekeeper.

"This generation—this 9/11 generation of soldiers, this new generation of scientists and advocates and entrepreneurs and altruists—you're the antidote to cynicism," Obama said. He urged graduates not to turn away from problems like climate change just because they are complex. "Cynicism has never won a war, or cured a disease, or started a business, or fed a young mind, or sent men into space," Obama said. "Cynicism is a choice. Hope is a better choice."

Student speakers shared his optimism. Jacqueline Rodriguez spoke about her father, who had fled war-torn El Salvador, and her mother, who had died from cancer when she was very young. The first in her family to finish high school and graduate from college, she completed a double major in sociology and Chicano/Latino studies and had been accepted into a PhD program in education. In the audience, her father wept with pride.

"It is up to our generation to continue providing these opportunities," Rodriguez said, "to continue our commitment to democracy and social justice as we are called to be doctors, lawyers, educators, policymakers or—and yes, I'm going to say it—the president of the United States."

▲ Early commencement
▶ ceremonies are so
intimate that the entire
graduating class and their
families could fit together
in Aldrich Park.

▲ *Today's graduates sport leis, stoles and decorated mortar boards with messages thanking Mom and Dad or expressing congratulations, such as "Si se pudo!"—"You did it!"*

▶ *Selfie stations at commencement 2014 proclaim love for UCI and are a sign of the times; tweeted messages and photos are posted on video boards at Angel Stadium.*

appendix

1. Founding and Current Administration

FOUNDING ADMINISTRATION 1965
Daniel G. Aldrich, Jr., chancellor
Richard L. Balch, vice chancellor student affairs
Jack W. Peltason, vice chancellor academic affairs
L.E. Cox, vice chancellor business and finance
John E. Smith, university librarian

FOUNDING DEANS 1965
Ralph Gerard, dean of graduate studies
Robert Mallough Saunders, dean of engineering
Richard C. Snyder, dean of the graduate school of administration
Richard N. Baisden, director of UC Extension at UC Irvine
Clayton Garrison, dean of the division of fine arts
Samuel Clyde McCulloch, dean of the division of humanities
James G. March, dean of the division of social sciences
Conway Pierce, assistant to the chancellor for physical sciences
Edward A. Steinhaus, dean of the division of biological sciences

CHANCELLOR'S CABINET 2014
Howard Gillman, chancellor
Michael Clark, interim provost and executive vice chancellor
Wendell Brase, vice chancellor, administrative and business services
John Hemminger, vice chancellor, research
Gregory Leet, vice chancellor university advancement
Meredith Michaels, vice chancellor planning and budget
Thomas A. Parham, vice chancellor, student affairs
Terry Belmont, CEO and associate vice chancellor for medical affairs
Kirsten Quanbeck, associate vice chancellor, equity, diversity, and inclusion
Ria Carlson, associate vice chancellor, strategic communications
Diane Geocaris, chief campus counsel
Ramona Agrela, associate chancellor
Michael Arias, associate chancellor
Roger Steinert, interim dean, school of medicine

DEANS 2014
Stephen Barker, interim, Claire Trevor School of the Arts
Frank LaFerla, Francisco J. Ayala School of Biological Sciences
Eric Spangenberg, Paul Merage School of Business
Deborah Vandell, School of Education
Frances Leslie, Graduate Division
Gregory Washington, Henry Samueli School of Engineering
Georges Van Den Abbeele, School of Humanities
Hal Stern, Donald Bren School of Information and Computer Sciences
Erwin Chemerinsky, UC Irvine School of Law
Roger Steinert, UC Irvine School of Medicine
Val Jenness, School of Social Ecology
Bill Maurer, School of Social Sciences
Michael Dennin, interim, Division of Undergraduate Education

2. UCI Foundation

EMERITI TRUSTEES
Arnold O. Beckman, Donald Bren, Joan Irvine Smith

TRUSTEES
Richard C. Ackerman, attorney at law | state senator (ret.), Ackerman Consulting
Amer A. Boukai '87, president, Continental Food Management
Richard K. Bridgford, partner, Bridgford, Gleason and Artinian | Attorneys at Law
Jane Buchan, CEO and managing director, Pacific Alternative Asset Management Co.
Paul E. Butterworth '81, executive vice president, engineering, You Technology, Inc.
Bruce E. Cahill, CEO, founder and chairman, Centaur Corporation
Hazem H. Chehabi, owner and president, Newport Diagnostic Center
Salma A. Chehabi '13, genetic counselor
D. Robinson Cluck '78, chairman and cofounder, Canterbury Consulting
Joseph L. Dunn, CEO, State Bar of California
John R. Evans, regional managing director (ret.), Wells Fargo Bank
Douglas K. Freeman, senior managing director, First Foundation Advisors
Edwin D. Fuller, president and CEO, The Group at Laguna
John D. Gerace '87, president and cofounder, Calabri Biosciences, LLC
Emile K. Haddad, president and CEO, FivePoint Communities
Raouf Y. Halim, CEO (ret.), Mindspeed Technologies
Julie N. Hill, director, WellPoint, Inc. | Lord Abbett
Phylis Y. Hsia, community leader
Gary H. Hunt, partner, California Strategies, LLC
Frank Jao, founder, chairman and CEO, Bridgecreek Group, Inc.

Steeve T. Kay, chairman, The Kay Family Foundation
Jack M. Langson, president, Investment Building Group
Mohannad S. Malas, founder and president, IRA Capital | Dana Investments
Charles D. Martin, chairman and CEO, Mont Pelerin Capital LLC
Fariborz Maseeh, managing principal, Picoco, LLC
James V. Mazzo, chairman and CEO, AcuFocus
Paul Merage, CEO and chairman, MIG Real Estate, LLC
Michael A. Mussallem, chairman and CEO, Edwards Lifesciences LLC
Eric Loren Nelson, consultant, Nelson Pharmaceutical Research
Dennis Luan Thuc Nguyen '94, chairman, New Asia Partners Limited
Thomas H. Nielsen, president, The Nielsen Company
James J. Peterson, chairman of the board and CEO, Microsemi Corporation
William F. Podlich, consulting managing director (ret.), Pacific Investment Management Co.
Cheryll R. Ruszat, executive director, Montessori Schools of Irvine
Richard J. Ruszat, president, Montessori Schools of Irvine
Michael Schulman, managing director, H and S Ventures, LLC
Gary J. Singer '74, senior advisor, RSI Holding Corporation
Ted Smith, chairman and CEO (ret.), MIND Research Institute
James Irvine Swinden, The Irvine Museum
Thomas T. Tierney, president, Vitatech Nutritional Sciences, Inc.
David L. Tsoong, chairman and president, Pinnacle Resources International, Inc.
Dean A. Yoost, managing partner (ret.), PricewaterhouseCoopers LLP
Thomas C. K. Yuen '74, chairman and CEO, Primegen Biotech L.L.C.

3. UCI Alumni Association Board

Bruce Hallett '78, president
John Gerace '87, president-elect

BOARD MEMBERS
Carol Choi '85
Justin Chung PhD '14
Robert Romney MS '83
Glen Kauffman '86, MBA '94
Kurt Busch '93
Salma Chehabi '99, '09, MS '13
Nick Desai '91
Gary Gorczyca '73
Neel Grover '92
Erin Gruwell '91
Maria Hall-Brown '84
John Hung '89, '90
Tim Kashani '86, MBA '91
Fred Sainick '74

Gary J. Singer '74
Jack Toan '94, MBA '02
William Um '90
Claudia White '89
James E. Wood Jr. MD '73

BOARD MEMBERS—ALUMNI CHAPTER REPRESENTATIVES
Andrew Chou '00
Katherine Hills '83
David Ochi '97, MBA '99

EX OFFICIO BOARD MEMBERS
Ramona Agrela, associate chancellor
Barney Elllis-Perry, assistant vice chancellor, alumni relations and CEO of the UCI Alumni Association
Sonali Madireddi, president, Associated Graduate Students
Reza Zomorrodian, president, Associated Students of UC Irvine
Monica Tran, president, Student Alumni Association

4. UCI Medal recipients

The Medal, UCI's highest honor, recognizes individuals who've made remarkable contributions to the university's mission, spirit and vision.

1984
Daniel G. Aldrich, Jr.

1987
Arnold O. Beckman
Athalie R. Clarke
Marianne McDonald '71

1988
Meryl Bonney
Robert B. Bonney
Walter B. Gerken
Abraham I. Melden

1989
Donald L. Bren
Richard P. Hausman
F. Sherwood Rowland
   (1995 Nobel Laureate)
Howard A. Schneiderman

1990
Roger W. Johnson
Murray Krieger
Mary W. Roosevelt
Elizabeth C. Tierney
Thomas T. Tierney
Thomas C.K. Yuen '74

Founders Award Recipients
Jean H. Aldrich
Edmund G. Brown
Edward W. Carter
Clark Kerr
Joan Irvine Smith

1992
James L. McGaugh

1993
Louise Turner Arnold
Robert S. Cohen
Martha F. Newkirk '81
Jack W. Peltason
Suzanne Peltason

1994
Michael W. Berns
Arlene Cheng
Eric L. Nelson
Dorothy M. Strauss '67

1995
Francisco J. Ayala
Thomas M. Keneally
Thomas H. Nielsen
Safi U. Qureshey
Marjorie T. Rawlins

1996
Peggy Goldwater Clay
David R. Dukes
William J. Gillespie
Louis A. Gottschalk
Yusef Komunyakaa '80

1998
The Chao Family
Spencer C. Olin
Michael P. Ramirez '84
Richard G. Sim

1999
Albert L. Nichols
Patricia W. Nichols
Norman Rostoker
Margaret L. Sprague
Robert R. Sprague

2000
William J. Lillyman
Donald McKayle
Ricardo Miledi
Henry Samueli
Susan Samueli

2001
Donald R. Beall
Joan F. Beall
George E. Hewitt
Meredith J. Khachigian
R. Duncan Luce
William F. Podlich III
Donald R. Beall
Joan F. Beall

2002
Jill Beck
Dwight W. Decker
J. Hillis Miller
Ted Smith

2003
Marian Bergeson
Philip Di Saia
Elizabeth and John Stahr

2004
Carl W. Cotman
Kingsley and John V. Croul
Robert Smith
Winifred Smith

2005
Thomas Cesario
Mary Cesario
Walter Fitch
Paul Merage
Janice Smith

2006
Julie Boyle
Douglas Freeman
Edward Shanbrom
Helen Shanbrom
Raymond Watson

2007
Gavin S. Herbert
Edward H. Newland
William Pereira

2008
Carol Cicerone
Ralph J. Cicerone
James Mazzo
Stanley van den Noort

2009
Anthony James
Fariborz Maseeh
William Parker
Laurel L. Wilkening

2010
Susan V. Bryant
Hazem Chehabi
Salma Chehabi '99
David Pyott
Scott Samuelsen

2011
Barbara Davidson ' 69
Manuel Gómez
Michael Mussallem
Larry Overman

2012
Bill Gross
Sue Gross
Elizabeth Loftus
David Tsoong
Betty Tu

2013
Charles D. Martin
Ngũgĩ wa Thiong'o
Cheryll Ruszat
Richard Ruszat

2014
Barack Obama

5. Lauds and Laurels Extraordinarius

The Extraordinarius award is conferred annually by the UCI Alumni Association in recognition of individuals
who have prominently contributed to the UCI campus and exemplify the spirit and purpose of the university.

Bernard Gelbaum, 1971	**James L. McGaugh**, 1982	**Susan Polan**, 1992	**Carol Cicerone**, 2003
Abraham Melden, 1972	**Mabry C. Steinhaus**, 1983	**Charles Lave**, 1993	**Joseph L. White**, 2004
Howard Schneiderman, 1973	**Jean Aldrich**, 1984	**Richard Everman**, 1994	**Alberto Manetta**, 2005
Ralph Gerard, 1974	**Thomas Cesario**, 1985	**Dick Sim**, 1995	**Spencer C. Olin**, 2006
Hazard Adams, 1975	**John Feltman**, 1986	**Patricia O'Brien**, 1996	**R. Duncan Luce**, 2007
Alexei Maradudin, 1976	**Marjorie C. Caserio**, 1987	**Roger W. Russell**, 1997	**Roy Dormaier**, 2008
L.E. Cox, 1977	**William J. Lillyman**, 1988	**Meredith J. Khachigian**, 1998	**James N. Danziger**, 2009
Michael P. Barris, 1978	**Arnold O. Beckman**, 1989	**Thomas and Elizabeth Tierney**, 1999	**Julian Feldman**, 2010
Gerald B. Sinykin, 1979	**William H. Parker**, 1989	**Jack & Suzanne Peltason**, 2000	**Brian Skyrms**, 2011
Daniel G. Aldrich, Jr., 1980	**Athalie R. Clarke**, 1990	**Glenn William Schaeffer**, 2001	**Michael R. Gottfredson**, 2012
Kivie Moldave, 1981	**John M. Whiteley**, 1991	**William R. Schonfeld**, 2002	**Edward Thorp**, 2013
			Thomas Yuen, 2014

6. Lauds and Laurels Past Recipients

J. Edward Berk, Community Service, 1971

Carolyn Watanabe, Community Service, 1971

Dia M. Dorsey, Distinguished Alumnus/Alumna, 1971

Morrie "Gale" Granger, Distinguished Research, 1971

Peter Colaclides, Distinguished Teaching, 1971

Bernard Gelbaum, Extraordinarius, 1971

Ferdi Massimino, Oustanding Student Athlete, 1971

John Halverson, Outstanding Senior, 1971

Ferdi Massimino, Outstanding Senior, 1971

Myron McNamara, Professional Achievement, 1971

Fred Engbarth, University Service, 1971

Bernard Gelbaum, University Service, 1971

Diana Janas, University Service, 1971

Richard Baisden, Community Service, 1972

UCI Associated Students, Community Service, 1972

Gene Uematsu, Community Service, 1972

Lynn Osen, Distinguished Alumnus/Alumna, 1972

Murray Krieger, Distinguished Research, 1972

Michael Butler, Distinguished Teaching, 1972

Abraham Melden, Extraordinarius, 1972

Phil Rhyne, Oustanding Student Athlete, 1972

Samuel Shacks, Outstanding Graduate Student, 1972

Gary Barrett, Outstanding Senior, 1972

Steve Chadima, Outstanding Senior, 1972

Betty Tesman, Professional Achievement, 1972

William Wadman III, Professional Achievement, 1972

Patrick Healey, University Service, 1972

Carol Heckman, University Service, 1972

Patrick Moore, University Service, 1972

Steve Feinberg, Community Service, 1973

Cliff Miller, Community Service, 1973

Robert L. Newcomb, Community Service, 1973

Kurt Snipes, Community Service, 1973

Alexei Maradudin, Distinguished Research, 1973

Nelson Pike, Distinguished Teaching, 1973

Howard Schneiderman, Extraordinarius, 1973

Jack Dickman, Oustanding Student Athlete, 1973

Lynn Humphreys, Outstanding Graduate Student, 1973

Tom Delapp, Outstanding Senior, 1973

Clayton Garrison, University Service, 1973

Helen Greening, University Service, 1973

Dori Nelson, University Service, 1973

Laureen Edwards Smith, University Service, 1973

Adreana Souleles, University Service, 1973

Education Movement, Community Service, 1974

La Escuelita, Community Service, 1974

John Lewin, Community Service, 1974

Gordon Marsh, Community Service, 1974

Jordan Phillips, Distinguished Alumnus/
Alumna, 1974

Louis Gottschalk, Distinguished Research, 1974

Marjorie C. Caserio, Distinguished Teaching, 1974

Ralph Gerard, Extraordinarius, 1974

Bob Chappell, Oustanding Student Athlete, 1974

Dirane Kelekyan, Outstanding Graduate Student, 1974

James Tait Goodrich, Outstanding Senior, 1974

Mary Dorothea Polk, Professional Achievement, 1974

Margaret Kravitz, University Service, 1974

Jay Martin, University Service, 1974

Evelyn Odell, University Service, 1974

John Rau, University Service, 1974

Ellene Sumner, University Service, 1974

Ron Huddleston, Community Service, 1975

Roland Schinzinger, Community Service, 1975

H. Colin Slim, Distinguished Research, 1975

Gary S. Lynch, Distinguished Teaching, 1975

Hazard Adams, Extraordinarius, 1975

Dave Baker, Oustanding Student Athlete, 1975

David Miller, Outstanding Graduate Student, 1975

William "Duffy" Michael, Outstanding Senior, 1975

Judy Jacobson, Professional Achievement, 1975

Eleanor Dorsey, University Service, 1975

Anton Ercegovich, University Service, 1975

Harry Le Grande, University Service, 1975

Gregory Scott Mills, University Service, 1975

Lyman W. Porter, University Service, 1975

Norman Weinberger, University Service, 1975

Robert S. Lawrence, Community Service, 1976

Judy B. Rosener, Community Service, 1976

Donnelen L. Sogn, Community Service, 1976

Cheryl F. Moore, Distinguished Alumnus/Alumna, 1976

F. Sherwood Rowland, Distinguished Research, 1976

Albert O. Wlecke, Distinguished Teaching, 1976

Alexei Maradudin, Extraordinarius, 1976

Tim Quinn, Oustanding Student Athlete, 1976

Shimon Eckhouse, Outstanding Graduate Student, 1976

Donald A. Frambach, Outstanding Senior, 1976

Gregory Scott Thomas, Outstanding Senior, 1976

Cynthia Johnson, Professional Achievement, 1976

J. Edward Berk, University Service, 1976

Norma J. Grundy, University Service, 1976

Bruce Scott Lavin, University Service, 1976

Paul Marx, University Service, 1976

Howard Lenhoff, Community Service, 1977

Gary Pivo, Community Service, 1977

Robert Taft, Distinguished Research, 1977

L.E. Cox, Extraordinarius, 1977

Steve Scott, Oustanding Student Athlete, 1977

Jerry J. Berge, Outstanding Graduate Student, 1977

Debra Peterson Dunn, Outstanding Senior, 1977

David Westrup, Outstanding Senior, 1977

Grace B. Bell, Professional Achievement, 1977

Warren L. Bostick, University Service, 1977

Robert R. Johnson, University Service, 1977

James B. Massey, University Service, 1977

David J.R. McCue, University Service, 1977

Mabry C. Steinhaus, University Service, 1977

Sylvia Hass Burlin, Community Service, 1978

Manuel N. Gomez, Community Service, 1978

Peter Odegard, Community Service, 1978

Robert Steedman, Distinguished Alumnus/Alumna, 1978

Kenneth Wexler, Distinguished Research, 1978

Calvin S. McLaughlin, Distinguished Teaching, 1978

Michael P. Barris, Extraordinarius, 1978

Lindsay Morse, Oustanding Student Athlete, 1978

Beverly A. Levi Eccles, Outstanding Graduate Student, 1978

Janet Brownstone, Outstanding Senior, 1978

John E. Connolly, Professional Achievement, 1978

Robert F. Gentry, Professional Achievement, 1978

Kathleen Calkins, University Service, 1978

C. Russell Duncan, University Service, 1978

Kenneth L. Kraemer, University Service, 1978

Frederick M. Linton, University Service, 1978

Jennifer Janz Merrilees, University Service, 1978

Carl H. Reinhart, University Service, 1978

Arnold Binder, Community Service, 1979

Joseph Spirito, Community Service, 1979

Vincent P. Carroll, Distinguished Alumnus/Alumna, 1979

Warren J. Hehre, Distinguished Research, 1979

Robert McIver, Distinguished Research, 1979

Larry E. Overman, Distinguished Research, 1979

James N. Danziger, Distinguished Teaching, 1979

Gerald B. Sinykin, Extraordinarius, 1979

Jeffrey K. Williams, Oustanding Student Athlete, 1979

Howard J. Gensler, Outstanding Senior, 1979

Stephen J. Blanchard, University Service, 1979

Masa K. Fujitani, University Service, 1979

Steve M. Kaplan, University Service, 1979

Cheryl F. Moore, University Service, 1979

Robert C. Warner, University Service, 1979

Robert N. Weed, University Service, 1979

Marlene M. Godoy, Community Service, 1980

Robert & Peggy Montgomery, Community Service, 1980

Harvey Williams, Community Service, 1980

Irving H. Leopold, Distinguished Research, 1980

Robert L. Newcomb, Distinguished Teaching, 1980

Daniel G. Aldrich, Jr., Extraordinarius, 1980

Evangelos Coskinas, Oustanding Student Athlete, 1980

Maryann Jacobi Gray, Outstanding Graduate Student, 1980

Cristi A. Wagenbach, Outstanding Senior, 1980

Kenneth P. Bailey, Professional Achievement, 1980

John A. Thorne, Professional Achievement, 1980

A. Benjamin Ehlert, University Service, 1980

Everly B. Fleischer, University Service, 1980

Dennis L. Hampton, University Service, 1980

Peggy Maradudin, University Service, 1980

William H. Parker, University Service, 1980

Janice L. Smith-Hill, University Service, 1980

Kurt A. Willis, University Service, 1980

Lawrence A. Rowe, Distinguished Alumnus/Alumna, 1981

Diane W. Wara, MD, Distinguished Alumnus/Alumna, 1981

Paul Sypherd, Distinguished Research, 1981

Carol Nance, Distinguished Staff Member, 1981

Catherine Smith, Distinguished Staff Member, 1981

Ermanno Bencivenga, Distinguished Teaching, 1981

John Rowe, Distinguished Teaching, 1981

Kivie Moldave, Extraordinarius, 1981

Molly L. Lynch, Outstanding Graduate Student, 1981

Cynthia Carlson, Outstanding Senior, 1981

Lillian Brown, Professional Achievement, 1981

Olga Maynard, Professional Achievement, 1981

Paul Arthur, University Service, 1981

Patrick Cadigan, University Service, 1981

Greeks, University Service, 1981

Carl Hartman, University Service, 1981

Ray Catalano, Community Service, 1982

Donald R. Sperling, Community Service, 1982

Mare Taagepera, Community Service, 1982

Harold Toliver, Distinguished Research, 1982

Maryann Jacobi Hall, Distinguished Staff Member, 1982

Helen Johnson, Distinguished Staff Member, 1982

Harold Moore, Distinguished Teaching, 1982

James McGaugh, Extraordinarius, 1982

Kevin Magee, Oustanding Student Athlete, 1982

LaVerne Brooks, Outstanding Senior, 1982

Craig Kauffman, Professional Achievement, 1982

James Tripodes, Professional Achievement, 1982

Gina Kelsch, University Service, 1982

Samuel Clyde McCulloch, University Service, 1982

Muriel Reynolds, University Service, 1982

Beverly "Babs" Sandeen, University Service, 1982

Randy Howatt, Distinguished Alumnus/Alumna, 1983

Guy De Mallac, Distinguished Research, 1983

Barbara L. Brown, Distinguished Staff Member, 1983

Jan Martin, Distinguished Staff Member, 1983

Franco Tonelli, Distinguished Teaching, 1983

Mabry C. Steinhaus, Extraordinarius, 1983

Peter Campbell, Oustanding Student Athlete, 1983

Kenneth M. Chomitz, Outstanding Graduate Student, 1983

Diane S. Tasaka, Outstanding Senior, 1983

Lois M. Corti, Professional Achievement, 1983

Philip J. DiSaia, Professional Achievement, 1983

Fred D. Henderson, University Service, 1983

Sumiyo E. Kastelic, University Service, 1983

Rev. William P. McLaughlin, University Service, 1983

Eloy Rodriguez, University Service, 1983

Larry E. Tenney, University Service, 1983

Randy H. Wold, University Service, 1983

Julia Banning, Community Service, 1984

Robert F. Gentry, Community Service, 1984

Jerry A. King, Distinguished Alumnus/Alumna, 1984

Douglas L. Mills, Distinguished Research, 1984

Carol K. Whalen, Distinguished Research, 1984

Wanda J. Cullers, Distinguished Staff Member, 1984

Michele K. Miller, Distinguished Staff Member, 1984

Viviane Wayne, Distinguished Staff Member, 1984

Margaret K. Murata, Distinguished Teaching, 1984

William R. Schonfeld, Distinguished Teaching, 1984

Jean Aldrich, Extraordinarius, 1984

Mark Ruelas, Oustanding Student Athlete, 1984

David G. Altman, Outstanding Graduate Student, 1984

Mai H. Nguyen, Outstanding Senior, 1984

Delores A. O'Brien, Outstanding Senior, 1984

Janet C. Loxley, Professional Achievement, 1984

Patti McKay, Professional Achievement, 1984

James H. Mulligan, Jr., Professional Achievement, 1984

Gay T. Iwamoto Akuni, University Service, 1984

William G. Gonzalez, University Service, 1984

Mary W. Roosevelt, University Service, 1984

Joseph Sandoval, Community Service, 1985

Johannes Van Vugt, Community Service, 1985

Douglas B. Davidson, Distinguished Alumnus/Alumna, 1985

Lyman W. Porter, Distinguished Research, 1985

Cynthia Eddleman, Distinguished Staff Member, 1985

Barbara LaChance, Distinguished Staff Member, 1985

Alice Macy, Distinguished Staff Member, 1985

Ed Petrillo, Distinguished Staff Member, 1985

Gary Evans, Distinguished Teaching, 1985

Thomas Cesario, Extraordinarius, 1985

Jim Gray, Oustanding Student Athlete, 1985

Julia Justus McGinity, Outstanding Senior, 1985

Michael Berns, Professional Achievement, 1985

Otto Reyer, Professional Achievement, 1985

Marianne Whitmyer, Professional Achievement, 1985

Margo Allen, University Service, 1985

Steve Armentrout, University Service, 1985

Joseph DiMento, University Service, 1985

Jim Kohlenberger, University Service, 1985

Thomas Nielsen, University Service, 1985

Steve Relyea, University Service, 1985

Dennis Lopez, Community Service, 1986

Chance Oberstein, Community Service, 1986

Mary Elizabeth Roth, Community Service, 1986

Thomas Yuen, Distinguished Alumnus/Alumna, 1986

Dennis Cunningham, Distinguished Research, 1986

John Hemminger, Distinguished Research, 1986

James B. Craig, Distinguished Staff Member, 1986

Linda Shattuck, Distinguished Staff Member, 1986

Jerry Wetsch, Distinguished Staff Member, 1986

Walter Wine, Distinguished Staff Member, 1986

Richard Barrutia, Distinguished Teaching, 1986

Thomas Crawford, Distinguished Teaching, 1986

John Feltman, Extraordinarius, 1986

Jeffrey Campbell, Oustanding Student Athlete, 1986

William Lambert, Outstanding Graduate Student, 1986

David MacDonald, Outstanding Senior, 1986

Cynthia Butler, Professional Achievement, 1986

Walter Henry, Professional Achievement, 1986

Hiroshi J. Ueha, Professional Achievement, 1986

Karin Zenk, Professional Achievement, 1986

Michael Butler, University Service, 1986

Barbara Davidson, University Service, 1986

Joan Friou, University Service, 1986

Leon Schwartz, University Service, 1986

Lois Sword, University Service, 1986

Ronald Wilson, University Service, 1986

Karen Bocard, Community Service, 1987

Ada Mae Hardeman, Community Service, 1987

Alfredo Morales, Community Service, 1987

Catherine Penny Sperling, Community Service, 1987

Willam A. Benbassat, Distinguished Alumnus/Alumna, 1987

Chen Tsai, Distinguished Research, 1987

William Drozda, Distinguished Staff Member, 1987

Millie Linn, Distinguished Staff Member, 1987

Charlotte London, Distinguished Staff Member, 1987

Patricia L. Price, Distinguished Staff Member, 1987

Casper W. Barnes, Distinguished Teaching, 1987

Olga Maynard, Distinguished Teaching, 1987

Marjorie C. Caserio, Extraordinarius, 1987

Scott Brooks, Oustanding Student Athlete, 1987

Mario Fajardo, Outstanding Graduate Student, 1987

Ronald Wek, Outstanding Graduate Student, 1987

William Caldarelli, Outstanding Senior, 1987

William E. Bunney, Jr., Professional Achievement, 1987

Ellen M. Lewis, Professional Achievement, 1987

Marianne Schnaubelt, Professional Achievement, 1987

Kevin Tremper, Professional Achievement, 1987

M. Arthur Charles, University Service, 1987

Todd Dickey, University Service, 1987

Randy Lewis, University Service, 1987

H. Wallace Merryman, University Service, 1987

Nell Mitchell, University Service, 1987

David Quisling, University Service, 1987

Gerald Weinstein, University Service, 1987

Peter Bowler, Community Service, 1988

Patricia Callahan, Community Service, 1988

Suzanne Martinez, Community Service, 1988

Diana Mercer, Community Service, 1988

Richard Ford, Distinguished Alumnus/Alumna, 1988

Eric Stanbridge, Distinguished Research, 1988

Penny Doff, Distinguished Staff Member, 1988

Elvira Schumacher, Distinguished Staff Member, 1988

Lillian "Sunny" Sundquist, Distinguished Staff Member, 1988

Mark Petracca, Distinguished Teaching, 1988

William J. Lillyman, Extraordinarius, 1988

Jill Harrington, Oustanding Student Athlete, 1988

Douglas Levine, Outstanding Graduate Student, 1988

Sanjay Saint, Outstanding Senior, 1988

John Brown, Professional Achievement, 1988

Theodore F. Brunner, Professional Achievement, 1988

Carla Espinoza, Professional Achievement, 1988

Rollin Randall, Professional Achievement, 1988

Barbara Bertin, University Service, 1988

Diane Nitta, University Service, 1988

Suzanne Peltason, University Service, 1988

Kym Salness, University Service, 1988

Dick Sim, University Service, 1988

Jennifer Tabola, University Service, 1988

Kogee Thomas, University Service, 1988

Patrick Hanratty, Distinguished Alumnus/Alumna, 1989

Gary S. Lynch, Distinguished Research, 1989

Westley J. Lagerberg, Distinguished Staff Member, 1989

Martha J. Levy, Distinguished Staff Member, 1989

Garland Parten, Distinguished Staff Member, 1989

Myron L. Braunstein, Distinguished Teaching, 1989

Arnold O. Beckman, Extraordinarius, 1989

William H. Parker, Extraordinarius, 1989

Mark Kaplan, Oustanding Student Athlete, 1989

Ted Scharf, Outstanding Graduate Student, 1989

Teri Ann Tracey, Outstanding Senior, 1989

Dianne A. Kane, Professional Achievement, 1989

Mare Taagepera, Professional Achievement, 1989

Roger Johnson, University Service, 1989

Juel Lee, University Service, 1989

Thomas & Elizabeth Tierney, University Service, 1989

Lucille Kuehn, Community Service, 1990

Sylvia Lenhoff, Community Service, 1990

George Miller, Community Service, 1990

Elaine Serra, Community Service, 1990

Thomas Garite, Distinguished Alumnus/Alumna, 1990

Edward Jones, Distinguished Research, 1990

George Ferrington, Distinguished Staff Member, 1990

Linda Bauer, Distinguished Teaching, 1990

Patrick Healey, Distinguished Teaching, 1990

Athalie R. Clarke, Extraordinarius, 1990

Christopher Duplanty, Oustanding Student Athlete, 1990

Shiraz Mishra, Outstanding Graduate Student, 1990

David J.R. Frakt, Outstanding Senior, 1990

John Miltner, Professional Achievement, 1990

Lonce Bailey, University Service, 1990

James Dunning, University Service, 1990

Jean Liechty, University Service, 1990

David Souleles, University Service, 1990

Elizabeth Stahr, University Service, 1990

John Stahr, University Service, 1990

Christian Werner, University Service, 1990

Jess Araujo, Community Service, 1991

Lynn Hammeras, Community Service, 1991

Kathy Smith White, Community Service, 1991

Martha Newkirk, Distinguished Alumnus/Alumna, 1991

Julio Torres, Distinguished Alumnus/Alumna, 1991

William E. Bunney, Jr., Distinguished Research, 1991

Nancy Anderson, Distinguished Staff Member, 1991

Teresa Camarillo, Distinguished Staff Member, 1991

Marcia Reed, Distinguished Staff Member, 1991

Karen Rook, Distinguished Teaching, 1991

Carlton Scott, Distinguished Teaching, 1991

John M. Whiteley, Extraordinarius, 1991

Elisabeth J. "Buffy" Rabbitt, Oustanding Student Athlete, 1991

Linda Matthei, Outstanding Graduate Student, 1991

Joseph Harris, Outstanding Senior, 1991

Robert Kazanjy, Professional Achievement, 1991

Robin Scarcella, Professional Achievement, 1991

Edra Brophy, University Service, 1991

Sandy Campbell, University Service, 1991

Jenny Doh, University Service, 1991

Joe & Melinda Huzsti, University Service, 1991

Christine Moseley, University Service, 1991

Eric Nelson, University Service, 1991

Spence Olin, University Service, 1991

Dorothy Strauss, University Service, 1991

Kimberly Ayala, Community Service, 1992

Elaine Hart, Community Service, 1992

Rein Taagepera, Community Service, 1992

Molly K. Lynch, Distinguished Alumnus/Alumna, 1992

Eileen Moore, Distinguished Alumnus/Alumna, 1992

T. Jefferson Parker, Distinguished Alumnus/Alumna, 1992

Maria Vigil, Distinguished Alumnus/Alumna, 1992

William Sirignano, Distinguished Research, 1992

Kathy Alberti, Distinguished Staff Member, 1992

Marti Barmore, Distinguished Staff Member, 1992

Dennis Ming, Distinguished Staff Member, 1992

Carol Tidwell, Distinguished Staff Member, 1992

Ollie Van Nostrand, Distinguished Staff Member, 1992

Leo Chavez, Distinguished Teaching, 1992

Patricia Hartz, Distinguished Teaching, 1992

Alberto Manetta, Distinguished Teaching, 1992

Susan Polan, Extraordinarius, 1992

Donald May, Oustanding Student Athlete, 1992

Xiangen Hu, Outstanding Graduate Student, 1992

Gina Marie Lichacz Hatheway, Outstanding Senior, 1992

Catherine Stites, Outstanding Senior, 1992

Donald McKayle, Professional Achievement, 1992

Mary Piccione, Professional Achievement, 1992

Ronald Young, Professional Achievement, 1992

Joan Ariel, University Service, 1992

Roy Dormaier, University Service, 1992

Jeni Duke, University Service, 1992

Betty Newcomb, University Service, 1992

Sally Peterson, University Service, 1992

Marjorie & Robert Rawlins, University Service, 1992

Laurie Bunnel, Community Service, 1993

Raul Magana, Community Service, 1993

Charles R. Pieper, Community Service, 1993

Jill Halvaks, Distinguished Alumnus/Alumna, 1993

Alfredo Ang, Distinguished Research, 1993

Julie Boyle, Distinguished Staff Member, 1993

Lynn Brown, Distinguished Staff Member, 1993

Ernie Holscher, Distinguished Staff Member, 1993

Donna Pattie, Distinguished Staff Member, 1993

Sandra Verdugo, Distinguished Staff Member, 1993

Mark Finkelstein, Distinguished Teaching, 1993

Michael Johnson, Distinguished Teaching, 1993

Charles Lave, Extraordinarius, 1993

Mike Hewitt, Oustanding Student Athlete, 1993

Beverly "Babs" Sandeen, Outstanding Graduate Student, 1993

Dean Matsubayashi, Outstanding Senior, 1993

Kenneth Baldwin, Professional Achievement, 1993

Lewis Bird, University Service, 1993

Christine Browning, University Service, 1993

Peggy Goldwater Clay, University Service, 1993

Kenneth Rohl, University Service, 1993

Robert Dean, Distinguished Alumnus/Alumna, 1994

William Batchelder, Distinguished Research, 1994

Marianne Bronner-Fraser, Distinguished Research, 1994

Marie Anderson, Distinguished Staff Member, 1994

Roberta Laible, Distinguished Staff Member, 1994

Essie Lev, Distinguished Staff Member, 1994

Rita Pitt, Distinguished Staff Member, 1994

A.J. Shaka, Distinguished Teaching, 1994

Richard Everman, Extraordinarius, 1994

Traci Goodrich Dorf, Oustanding Student Athlete, 1994

Mark Calkins, Outstanding Graduate Student, 1994

Nguyen-Hong Hoang, Outstanding Senior, 1994

Matthew Siler, Outstanding Senior, 1994

Ricardo Asch, Professional Achievement, 1994

Marie T. Pezzlo, Professional Achievement, 1994

Gloria Gellman, University Service, 1994

Mary-Louise Kean, University Service, 1994

Mela Miledi, University Service, 1994

Hoda Anton-Culver, Community Service, 1995

Jon Lovitz, Distinguished Alumnus/Alumna, 1995

Salvador Sarmiento, Distinguished Alumnus/Alumna, 1995

David Easton, Distinguished Research, 1995

Christine M. Gall, Distinguished Research, 1995

DeWayne Green, Distinguished Staff Member, 1995

Karl Wolonsky, Distinguished Staff Member, 1995

William Heidbrink, Distinguished Teaching, 1995

Dick Sim, Extraordinarius, 1995

Khalid Channell, Oustanding Student Athlete, 1995

Alison Holman, Outstanding Graduate Student, 1995

Monique Viengkhou, Outstanding Senior, 1995

Bernard Grofman, Professional Achievement, 1995

Herb Spiwak, Professional Achievement, 1995

Thomas Cesario, University Service, 1995

Edward Schumacher, University Service, 1995

George Brauel, Community Service, 1996

Tiffany Haugen, Community Service, 1996

Ramon Munoz, Distinguished Alumnus/Alumna, 1996

Jamie Trevor, Distinguished Alumnus/Alumna, 1996

Janos Lanyi, Distinguished Research, 1996

Candice Garretson, Distinguished Staff Member, 1996

RuAnn Watson, Distinguished Staff Member, 1996

Luci Berkowitz, Distinguished Teaching, 1996

Edward Dana, Distinguished Teaching, 1996

Patricia O'Brien, Extraordinarius, 1996

Allah-mi Basheer, Oustanding Student Athlete, 1996

Rebecca Martinez, Outstanding Graduate Student, 1996

Anh Ludi Ngo, Outstanding Senior, 1996

Frank Cancian, University Service, 1996

Kate Maxey, University Service, 1996

Jesse Bueno, Distinguished Alumnus/Alumna, 1997

Stephen M. Silverman, Distinguished Alumnus/Alumna, 1997

David A. Brant, Distinguished Teaching, 1997

Roger W. Russell, Extraordinarius, 1997

Skye Green, Oustanding Student Athlete, 1997

Anne McInnis, Outstanding Community Friend, 1997

Jim & Madeline Swinden, Outstanding Community Friend, 1997

Linda Schechinger, Outstanding Graduate Student, 1997

Jennifer E. Cole Gutierrez, Outstanding Senior, 1997

Ellen Broidy, Staff Achievement, 1997

Fawzi Hermez, Staff Achievement, 1997

Ted Smith, Community Service, 1998

Tamerou Asrat, Distinguished Alumnus/Alumna, 1998

Brian Cooper, Distinguished Alumnus/Alumna, 1998

Erin Gruwell, Distinguished Alumnus/Alumna, 1998

Russell Lande, Distinguished Alumnus/Alumna, 1998

Wayne Lowell, Distinguished Alumnus/Alumna, 1998

Howard Murad, Distinguished Alumnus/Alumna, 1998

Gary Singer, Distinguished Alumnus/Alumna, 1998

Donna Soto-Morettini, Distinguished Alumnus/Alumna, 1998

Meredith Khachigian, Extraordinarius, 1998

Richard A. Hill, Faculty Achievement, 1998

Leticia Oseguera, Oustanding Student Athlete, 1998

Nira K. Roston, Outstanding Community Friend, 1998

Lionel Cantu, Outstanding Graduate Student, 1998

Alexander Frid, Outstanding Undergraduate, 1998

John S. Clarke, Staff Achievement, 1998

Stephen Matthews, University Service, 1998

Toni Alexander, Distinguished Alumnus/Alumna, 1999

Aimee Bender, Distinguished Alumnus/Alumna, 1999

Carl V. Fields, Distinguished Alumnus/Alumna, 1999

Rudy Hanley, Distinguished Alumnus/Alumna, 1999

David Kim, Distinguished Alumnus/Alumna, 1999

Dorothy Marsh, Distinguished Alumnus/Alumna, 1999

Julia Justus McGinity, Distinguished Alumnus/Alumna, 1999

Larry E. Tenney, Distinguished Alumnus/Alumna, 1999

Thomas & Elizabeth Tierney, Extraordinarius, 1999

Nostratola "Nick" Vaziri, Faculty Achievement, 1999

Nicole Bucciarelli, Oustanding Student Athlete, 1999

Walter Gerken, Outstanding Community Friend, 1999

Rick Grannis, Outstanding Graduate Student, 1999

Mei Mei Peng, Outstanding Undergraduate, 1999

Elizabeth Toomey, Staff Achievement, 1999

Kenneth W. Bentley, Distinguished Alumnus/Alumna, 2000

Kenneth Charlton, Distinguished Alumnus/Alumna, 2000

Frank Lynch, Distinguished Alumnus/Alumna, 2000

Lisa Stephenson Mills, Distinguished Alumnus/Alumna, 2000

Siegfried Heinz Reich, Distinguished Alumnus/Alumna, 2000

David Scott Silver, Distinguished Alumnus/Alumna, 2000

Brian Thompson, Distinguished Alumnus/Alumna, 2000

Moises Torres, Distinguished Alumnus/Alumna, 2000

Jack and Suzanne Peltason, Extraordinarius, 2000

John D. Dombrink, Faculty Achievement, 2000

Frank Meyskens, Jr., Faculty Achievement, 2000

Marek Ondera, Oustanding Student Athlete, 2000

Maria G. Rendon, Oustanding Student Athlete, 2000

George E. and Doretha Hewitt, Outstanding Community Friend, 2000

Roy Thomas Fielding, Outstanding Graduate Student, 2000

Raschel Greenberg, Staff Achievement, 2000

Enid Acosta-Tello, Distinguished Alumnus/Alumna, 2001

Brian G. Atwood, Distinguished Alumnus/Alumna, 2001

David L. Bernick, Distinguished Alumnus/Alumna, 2001

Jonathon Dorfan, Distinguished Alumnus/Alumna, 2001

Bruce Robert Hallett, Distinguished Alumnus/Alumna, 2001

Daniel C. Hedigan, Distinguished Alumnus/Alumna, 2001

Diana M. Leach, Distinguished Alumnus/Alumna, 2001

Mark Braden Moore, Distinguished Alumnus/Alumna, 2001

Jeffrey Prostor, Distinguished Alumnus/Alumna, 2001

Alex Razmjoo, Distinguished Alumnus/Alumna, 2001

Andrew E. Senyei, Distinguished Alumnus/Alumna, 2001

Glenn William Schaeffer, Extraordinarius, 2001

Bernard Grofman, Faculty Achievement, 2001

Kareen Nilsson, Oustanding Student Athlete, 2001

Joyce A. Tucker, Outstanding Community Friend, 2001

Anne Dow, Outstanding Graduate Student, 2001

Han Kang, Outstanding Undergraduate, 2001

Michael Arias, Staff Achievement, 2001

JoAnn Aguirre, Distinguished Alumnus/Alumna, 2002

Thomas C. Bent, Distinguished Alumnus/Alumna, 2002

John A. Creelman, Distinguished Alumnus/Alumna, 2002

Joseph Lacob, Distinguished Alumnus/Alumna, 2002

Marianne McDonald, Distinguished Alumnus/Alumna, 2002

Richard Gordon Miller, Distinguished Alumnus/Alumna, 2002

Paul Mockapetris, Distinguished Alumnus/Alumna, 2002

David Ritchie, Distinguished Alumnus/Alumna, 2002

Beverly "Babs" Sandeen, Distinguished Alumnus/Alumna, 2002

Christopher Schott, Distinguished Alumnus/Alumna, 2002

William R. Schonfeld, Extraordinarius, 2002

Barbara Burgess, Faculty Achievement, 2002

Cindy Oparah, Oustanding Student Athlete, 2002

Douglas K. Freeman, Outstanding Community Friend, 2002

Kimberley Coles, Outstanding Graduate Student, 2002

Leah Donahue, Outstanding Undergraduate, 2002

Tina Arth, Staff Achievement, 2002

Steven R. Angle, Distinguished Alumnus/Alumna, 2003

Steven R. Borowski, Distinguished Alumnus/Alumna, 2003

Maureen Burns, Distinguished Alumnus/Alumna, 2003

Darcy & Richard Kopcho, Distinguished Alumnus/Alumna, 2003

Tina Nova, Distinguished Alumnus/Alumna, 2003

William D. Parham, Distinguished Alumnus/Alumna, 2003

Carlos Prietto, Distinguished Alumnus/Alumna, 2003

Marshall Rose, Distinguished Alumnus/Alumna, 2003

Eric Shen, Distinguished Alumnus/Alumna, 2003

LaVonne Smith, Distinguished Alumnus/Alumna, 2003

Carol Cicerone, Extraordinarius, 2003

Dan Stokols, Faculty Achievement, 2003

Scott Bowman, Oustanding Student Athlete, 2003

Jon Wampler, Outstanding Community Friend, 2003

Mario San Bartolome, Outstanding Graduate Student, 2003

Steven G. Ortiz, Outstanding Undergraduate, 2003

Amy Shively, Outstanding Undergraduate, 2003

Thomas Parham, Staff Achievement, 2003

Kris Elftmann, Community Service, 2004

Gregory A. Bolcer, Distinguished Alumnus/Alumna, 2004

Kimberly B. Burge, Distinguished Alumnus/Alumna, 2004

Deborah Daniel, Distinguished Alumnus/Alumna, 2004

Anthony A. James, Distinguished Alumnus/Alumna, 2004

James Largent, Distinguished Alumnus/Alumna, 2004

Christopher Lundquist, Distinguished Alumnus/Alumna, 2004

Wesley D. Motooka, Distinguished Alumnus/Alumna, 2004

K. Mark Nelson, Distinguished Alumnus/Alumna, 2004

Steven Rodriguez, Distinguished Alumnus/Alumna, 2004

Jose Solorio, Distinguished Alumnus/Alumna, 2004

Jospeh L. White, Extraordinarius, 2004

Robert G. Moeller, Faculty Achievement, 2004

Jimmy Pelzel, Oustanding Student Athlete, 2004

Celine Jacquemin, Outstanding Graduate Student, 2004

Brad R. Cohn, Outstanding Undergraduate, 2004

Annette R. Luckow, Staff Achievement, 2004

Carole Nightengale, Staff Achievement, 2004

Patricia Beckman, Community Service, 2005

Pamela Adams, Distinguished Alumnus/Alumna, 2005

Paul Butterworth, Distinguished Alumnus/Alumna, 2005

Curt Campbell, Distinguished Alumnus/Alumna, 2005

Maria Hall-Brown, Distinguished Alumnus/Alumna, 2005

Peggy Maradudin, Distinguished Alumnus/Alumna, 2005

Martin Morris, Distinguished Alumnus/Alumna, 2005

Kathie Lynn Olsen, Distinguished Alumnus/Alumna, 2005

Rob Peirson, Distinguished Alumnus/Alumna, 2005

Steve Scott, Distinguished Alumnus/Alumna, 2005

Brian Wandell, Distinguished Alumnus/Alumna, 2005

Alberto Manetta, Extraordinarius, 2005

Elizabeth Loftus, Faculty Achievement, 2005

Ashlie Hain, Oustanding Student Athlete, 2005

Yvonne Braun, Outstanding Graduate Student, 2005

Jacqueline Chattopadhayay, Outstanding Undergraduate, 2005

Marjorie DeMartino, Staff Achievement, 2005

Audrey DeVore, Staff Achievement, 2005

Vanessa Zuabi, Community Service, 2006

Roger Lewis Bratcher, Distinguished Alumnus/Alumna, 2006

William Butler, Distinguished Alumnus/Alumna, 2006

Michael Chabon, Distinguished Alumnus/Alumna, 2006

Jenn Colella, Distinguished Alumnus/Alumna, 2006

David Dimas, Distinguished Alumnus/Alumna, 2006

John E. Edwards, Jr., Distinguished Alumnus/Alumna, 2006

Steven Joe, Distinguished Alumnus/Alumna, 2006

Beth Malone, Distinguished Alumnus/Alumna, 2006

David Marrero, Distinguished Alumnus/Alumna, 2006

Nick Scandone, Distinguished Alumnus/Alumna, 2006

Jeffrey Thomas Yuen, Distinguished Alumnus/Alumna, 2006

Spencer C. Olin, Extraordinarius, 2006

Ross Schraeder, Oustanding Student Athlete, 2006

Bryan McDonald, Outstanding Graduate Student, 2006

Vivek Mehta, Outstanding Undergraduate, 2006

Said M. Shokair, Staff Achievement, 2006

Ellen D. Schlosser, Community Service, 2007

David G. Altman, Distinguished Alumnus/Alumna, 2007

Sharon L. Cordes, Distinguished Alumnus/Alumna, 2007

James Tait Goodrich, Distinguished Alumnus/Alumna, 2007

Patrick P. Hong, Distinguished Alumnus/Alumna, 2007

Dennis C. Jacobs, Distinguished Alumnus/Alumna, 2007

Stephanie Marie Powell, Distinguished Alumnus/Alumna, 2007

Fred Sainick, Distinguished Alumnus/Alumna, 2007

Betty K. Tu, Distinguished Alumnus/Alumna, 2007

Brett J. Willamson, Distinguished Alumnus/Alumna, 2007

R. Duncan Luce, Extraordinarius, 2007

Kenneth Small, Faculty Achievement, 2007

Jayson Michael Jablonsky, Oustanding Student Athlete, 2007

Brook Haley, Outstanding Graduate Student, 2007

Marlen M. Kanagui, Outstanding Undergraduate, 2007

Stacie J. Tibbetts, Staff Achievement, 2007

Sasha Strauss, Community Service, 2008

Jill Bolton, Distinguished Alumnus/Alumna, 2008

Ed Low Chang, Distinguished Alumnus/Alumna, 2008

Christine Dormaier, Distinguished Alumnus/Alumna, 2008

Phillip Robert Fischer, MD, Distinguished Alumnus/Alumna, 2008

Ted Walker Kryzczko, Distinguished Alumnus/Alumna, 2008

Leon S. LaPorte, Distinguished Alumnus/Alumna, 2008

Goran Matijasevic, PhD, Distinguished Alumnus/Alumna, 2008

Joan Petersilia, PhD, Distinguished Alumnus/Alumna, 2008

Robert Pletka, EdD, Distinguished Alumnus/Alumna, 2008

Nancy Kim Yun, Distinguished Alumnus/Alumna, 2008

Roy Dormaier, Extraordinarius, 2008

Michael J. Prather, Faculty Achievement, 2008

Tim Hutten, Oustanding Student Athlete, 2008

Roberto Gonzales, Outstanding Graduate Student, 2008

Jenna Otter, Outstanding Undergraduate, 2008

Susen Csikesz, Staff Achievement, 2008

John Speraw, Staff Achievement, 2008

Pamela A. Kelley, Community Service, 2009

Colette Atkinson, Distinguished Alumnus/Alumna, 2009

Rudolph Baldoni, Distinguished Alumnus/Alumna, 2009

Roy Beven, Distinguished Alumnus/Alumna, 2009

Daniel Boehne, Distinguished Alumnus/Alumna, 2009

Samuel W. Downing, Distinguished Alumnus/Alumna, 2009

David Feign, Distinguished Alumnus/Alumna, 2009

Christina Giguiere, Distinguished Alumnus/Alumna, 2009

Mary Jo Lang, Distinguished Alumnus/Alumna, 2009

Lisa Stephenson Locklear, Distinguished Alumnus/Alumna, 2009

Jose Solorio, Distinguished Alumnus/Alumna, 2009

John Tracy, Distinguished Alumnus/Alumna, 2009

James N. Danziger, Extraordinarius, 2009

Donald Blake, Faculty Achievement, 2009

Jon Steller, Oustanding Student Athlete, 2009

Kathy Rim, Outstanding Graduate Student, 2009

Ali Malik, Outstanding Undergraduate, 2009

David Leinen, Staff Achievement, 2009

Dulcie and Larry Kugelman, Community Service, 2010

Robert Burk, Distinguished Alumnus/Alumna, 2010

Sheila Schuller Coleman, Distinguished Alumnus/Alumna, 2010

Jenny Doh, Distinguished Alumnus/Alumna, 2010

Manuel Gomez, Distinguished Alumnus/Alumna, 2010

Rebecca Grinter, Distinguished Alumnus/Alumna, 2010

Atsushi Horiba, Distinguished Alumnus/Alumna, 2010

George Kessinger, Distinguished Alumnus/Alumna, 2010

Maria Minon, Distinguished Alumnus/Alumna, 2010

Dennis Nguyen, Distinguished Alumnus/Alumna, 2010

Sheldon S. Zinberg, Distinguished Alumnus/Alumna, 2010

Julian Feldman, Extraordinarius, 2010

Roger McWilliams, Faculty Achievement, 2010

Lauren Collins, Oustanding Student Athlete, 2010

Chris Stout, Outstanding Graduate Student, 2010

Megan Braun, Outstanding Undergraduate, 2010

Cindy Sasso, Staff Achievement, 2010

Judi Conroy, Distinguished Alumnus/Alumna, 2011

Paramesh Gopi, Distinguished Alumnus/Alumna, 2011

Katherine Hills, Distinguished Alumnus/Alumna, 2011

Shelley Hoss, Distinguished Alumnus/Alumna, 2011

Richard Kammerman, Distinguished Alumnus/Alumna, 2011

David MacMillan, Distinguished Alumnus/Alumna, 2011

Joan Patronite Kelly, Distinguished Alumnus/Alumna, 2011

Scott Steiner, Distinguished Alumnus/Alumna, 2011

Jon Teichrow, Distinguished Alumnus/Alumna, 2011

Hector Tobar, Distinguished Alumnus/Alumna, 2011

Teal Wicks, Distinguished Alumnus/Alumna, 2011

Brian Skyrms, Extraordinarius, 2011

Bill Maurer, Faculty Achievement, 2011

Tanya Taylor, Oustanding Student Athlete, 2011

Daisy Verduzco Reyes, Outstanding Graduate Student, 2011

Michael Nguyen, Outstanding Undergraduate, 2011

Helen Morgan, Staff Achievement, 2011

Richard and Cheryll Ruszat, University Service, 2011

Nadia Bermudez, Distinguished Alumnus/Alumna, 2012

Al De Grassi, Distinguished Alumnus/Alumna, 2012

Channing Der, Distinguished Alumnus/Alumna, 2012

Peter Fischler, Distinguished Alumnus/Alumna, 2012

John C. Hemminger, Distinguished Alumnus/Alumna, 2012

Victor Passy, Distinguished Alumnus/Alumna, 2012

Walt Scacchi, Distinguished Alumnus/Alumna, 2012

Everardo Stanton, Distinguished Alumnus/Alumna, 2012

Truc Vu, Distinguished Alumnus/Alumna, 2012

Terrance Walker, Distinguished Alumnus/Alumna, 2012

Darren Wilsey, Distinguished Alumnus/Alumna, 2012

Michael R. Gottfredson, Extraordinarius, 2012

David A. Snow, Faculty Achievement, 2012

James A. Newkirk, Honorary Alumni, 2012

Charles Jock, Oustanding Student Athlete, 2012

James Weatherall, Outstanding Graduate Student, 2012

Armaan Rowther, Outstanding Undergraduate, 2012

Sue K. Marshall, Staff Achievement, 2012

Daniel G. Aldrich III, University Service, 2012

Janice Cimbalo, Distinguished Alumnus/Alumna, 2013

Richard Cote, Distinguished Alumnus/Alumna, 2013

Keith Curry, Distinguished Alumnus/Alumna, 2013

Georgina Dodge, Distinguished Alumnus/Alumna, 2013

Gregory Lai, Distinguished Alumnus/Alumna, 2013

Karen Noblett, Distinguished Alumnus/Alumna, 2013

Daniel Russell, Distinguished Alumnus/Alumna, 2013

Ted Scharf, Distinguished Alumnus/Alumna, 2013

Krishna Shenoy, Distinguished Alumnus/Alumna, 2013

Richard Thompson, Distinguished Alumnus/Alumna, 2013

Toby Weiner, Distinguished Alumnus/Alumna, 2013

Edward Thorp, Extraordinarius, 2013

Arthur Lander, Faculty Achievement, 2013

Kevin Tillie, Oustanding Student Athlete, 2013

Victoria Lowerson, Outstanding Graduate Student, 2013

Pichaya Kositsawat, Outstanding Undergraduate, 2013

Luis Bravo-Mota, Outstanding University Service, 2013

Michael Poston, Staff Achievement, 2013

Luis Mota-Bravo, University Service, 2013

Arif Alikhan, Distinguished Alumnus/Alumna, 2014

Ami Bera, Distinguished Alumnus/Alumna, 2014

James Patrick Berney, Distinguished Alumnus/Alumna, 2014

Shimon Eckhouse, Distinguished Alumnus/Alumna, 2014

Steven Keller, Distinguished Alumnus/Alumna, 2014

Jackie Lacey, Distinguished Alumnus/Alumna, 2014

Steven Lam, Distinguished Alumnus/Alumna, 2014

Taryn Rose, Distinguished Alumnus/Alumna, 2014

Douglas Thorpe, Distinguished Alumnus/Alumna, 2014

Jack Toan, Distinguished Alumnus/Alumna, 2014

Carl Ware, Distinguished Alumnus/Alumna, 2014

Colin Andrews, Distinguished Staff Member, 2014

Thomas Yuen, Extraordinarius, 2014

Barbara Dosher, Faculty Achievement, 2014

Michael V. Drake, Honorary Alumni, 2014

Mitch Wise, Oustanding Student Athlete, 2014

Sandra Holden, Outstanding Graduate Student, 2014

Sasha Sabherwal, Outstanding Undergraduate, 2014

Frank LaFerla, University Service, 2014

photo credits

Due diligence has been exercised to identify and acknowledge rights ownership of all content in this book. Should anyone have further information about rights or attribution, please contact the publisher or UC Irvine.

Images identified by page reference here are either copyright to or the property of the persons or institutions listed. Photographers for UCI Archives over the years include: Tom Carroll, Garth Chandler, Wayne A. Clark, Judy Cohen, T. Cooper, Stuart Droker, Arthur Dubinsky, Anton Ercegovich, Beth Koch, Rene Laursen, William Laird, J. Eric Lawrence, John Malmin, Clay Miller, William Miller, Stuart Shaffer, Bertil Svensson, Ted Streshinsky and Tom F. Walters.

The following images appear in alphabetical order:

34, 37 (L), 40 (TL), 40–41, 47 (BR), 51 (L), 52, 53 (TL) (B), 54 (T) (R), 55 (T), 65 (L), 74, 75 (T) **Ansel Adams, UCR/ California Museum of Photography, Sweeney/Rubin Ansel Adams FIAT LUX Collection, University of California, Riverside**; 30, 31 (B), 44 (L), 69 (B), 82, 83 (B), 108–109 (T), 114, 127 (TL), 130–131, 132–133, 139 (L), 146 (B) **Daniel A. Anderson**; 143 **Photo/illustration by Daniel A. Anderson and Hoang Xuan Pham**; 7 (B), 28, 33, 36 (L), 36–37, 43 (T), 44–45, 45, 46, 46–47, 47 (TL) (TR), 48 (R), 49, 50 (TL) (TR) (BL), 51 (R), 56, 56–57, 64 (T), 65 (R), 66–67, 71 (T), 72, 75 (BL) (BR), 76, 78–79, 79, 80 (B), 81 (B), 86 (TL) (TR), 86–87, 92 (TL) (TR), 93, 94 (T) (L), 95 (T) (R), 96 (BL), 96–97, 103, 106, 110, 111, 112–113, 115 (TR), 116, 118, 118–119, 124–125, 126, 128 (T) (L), 129, 130 (T) (L), 134, 135, 136–137, 138–139, 139 (R), 142 (BL) (BR), 145 (L), 147 **Julian Andrews**; 152 (L) **Courtesy of Ami Bera**; 128–129 **Courtesy of Campus Recreation**; 155 (T), 157 (R) **Gilberto Cardenas**; 141 (TL) (TR) (L) **Nicole del Castillo, Luke Hegel-Cantarella**; 117 (T) (M) (R) (BL) **Claudia Cheffs**; 34–35 **Donald Flamm, Philco-Ford Aeronutronic/UCI Archives**; 121 (TR) **Focus on Sport/Getty Images**; 152 (R) **Courtesy of Jeanine Hill**; 156–157 **Laurel Hungerford**; 140 (B) **Courtesy of Ivey Entertainment**; 58–59, 92 (B) **Paul Kennedy**; 124 (BL), 151 (R) **Michelle S. Kim**; 73 (BL) **Beth Koch/UCI Archives**; 142 (L) **Courtesy of Laguna College of Art and Design**; 149–149 **Jocelyn Lee**; 86 (BL) **Nick Merrick**; 85 **Henrik Montgomery/AFP/Getty Images**; 152 (T) **Courtesy of Janet Nguyen**; 162 **Christopher James Nugent**; 55 (BR) **Hoang Xuan Pham**; 159 (B) **Carlos Puma**; 38–39 (T) **Richard Schlesinger/ UCI Archives**; 29 (B) **Eveline Shih-Pitcairn/Photo Boutique**; 12 **Courtesy of James Irvine Swinden**; 124 (TR) **Wayne Tilcock**; 14 **TIME Magazine©, September 6, 1963, Time Inc.**; 2–3 **Courtesy of UC Regents**; 4, 6, 7 (TL) (TR), 8, 8–9, 10, 11, 13, 15 (R), 16, 16–17, 17, 18–19, 20, 20–21, 21, 22, 22–23, 24, 25, 26 (T) (R), 27, 29 (T) (M), 36 (T) (M), 37 (M) (R), 38 (L), 38–39 (B), 39, 40 (BL) (BR), 41, 42 (B), 43, 48 (BL), 53 (TR), 54 (T), 55 (L), 60, 60–61, 62, 62–63, 63, 64 (B), 67, 68, 70, 70–71, 73 (TL) (TR) (M) (BM) (BR), 77 (B), 78 (B), 80 (L), 83 (T), 84, 90 (L), 94 (R), 95 (L), 96 (TL), 98, 98–99, 100, 101, 102, 102–103, 104 (TL) (TR) (L) (B), 105 (T), 107, 108–109 (B), 109, 115 (TL), 120, 120–121, 121 (BL), 122, 131, 136, 142 (TL) (TR), 144, 144–145, 150 (T), 151 (T), 158 **UC Irvine Libraries, Special Collections and Archives**; 121 (BR), 123, 124 (TL) (L) (BL), 125, 127 **Courtesy of UCI Athletics**; 15 (L), 26 (L), 42–43, 44 (R), 48 (T), 141 (B), 148, 149 (T) **UCI Strategic Communications**; 117 (L) **Daniel Wehrenfennig**; 89 **Iris Yokoi**; 113 **Aaron Young**; 31 (T), 32, 50 (BR), 69 (T), 77 (T), 81 (T), 82–83, 87, 88, 90–91, 91, 104 (M), 105 (B), 115 (B), 119 (B), 132 (L), 133, 138, 140 (TL) (TR), 145 (R), 146 (T), 149 (B), 150–151, 153, 154, 156 (L) (R), 157 (B)(TM), 159 (T), 170 **Steve Zylius**

169

acknowledgments

UC Irvine: Bright Past, Brilliant Future was made possible through the dedicated collaboration of campus personnel and supporters. So many people who value the University of California, Irvine and its contributions to the community have given their knowledge and expertise to provide a clear understanding of the campus history, its place in the community today and its path to the future.

Key to our research was the UCI Libraries Special Collections and Archives under University Librarian Lorelei Tanji and Assistant University Librarian John Renaud. We are grateful to tireless sleuths Christine Kim, Steve MacLeod, Laura Uglean Jackson, Krystal Tribbett and Audra Eagle Yun, head of special collections and archives. Interviews of founding faculty and administrators by Samuel Clyde McCulloch proved invaluable. UCI Athletics staff Fumi Kimura, Bob Olson and Stacey Shackleford dug deep into their files for photos and information on sports history. Leigh Gleason, curator of California Museum of Photography at UC Riverside facilitated access to Ansel Adams' photos. Many thanks also to James Swinden who allowed us to tap his family photo collection and to Ellen Bell of the Irvine Historical Society.

Thanks also go to Chancellor Michael V. Drake, who first recognized the merit of this project in fall 2012, and to Meredith Michaels, vice chancellor of planning and budget, who authorized the funding.

Writers Sharon L. Roan and John Westcott worked under tight deadlines to produce smart and interesting stories. Their flexibility and cooperation is much appreciated.

Writers received gracious cooperation from a long roster of interviewees: Larry Agran, City of Irvine; Charlie Brande, alumnus and former women's volleyball coach; Wendell Brase, vice chancellor administrative and business services; Megan Braun, UCI's first Rhodes Scholar; Scott Brooks '87, sponsor of the annual Scott Brooks Golf Tournament funding UCI athletic scholarships and current coach of NBA Division Title winning Oklahoma Thunder; Michael Burton, anthropology professor; Justin Chung, former Associated Graduate Students president; Ralph J. Cicerone, fourth UC Irvine Chancellor; Steven Choi, Irvine mayor; Michael Clark, interim provost and executive vice chancellor; Robert Cohen, founding faculty member in drama; Richard Demerjian, director of environmental planning and sustainability; Michael V. Drake, fifth UCI Chancellor; Howard Gillman, current UC Irvine Chancellor; Rebekah Gladson, campus architect; Manuel Gomez, retired vice chancellor student affairs; James L. McGaugh, founding faculty member in neurobiology and behavior; Paul Merage, chair of the executive committee of the dean's advisory board of the Paul Merage School of Business; Keith Nelson, founding professor of history; Ted Newland, longtime men's water polo coach; Spencer C. Olin, founding faculty member in history; Bob Olson, associate athletic director, media relations; Thomas Parham, vice chancellor student affairs; William Parker, professor emeritus physics and astronomy; Joan Irvine Smith, great-granddaughter of James Irvine; Liz Toomey, daughter of founding Chancellor Daniel G. Aldrich, Jr. and recently retired assistant vice chancellor for community and government relations; Daniel Wehrenfennig, director Olive Tree Initiative; and Joseph L. White, professor emeritus, social sciences.

The anniversary book advisory committee kept the project moving forward and provided valuable feedback. Members include: Kathryn Bold, Ria Carlson, Michael Clark, Edgar Dormitorio, Stephanie Fix, Jeri Frederick, Daniel Montplaisir, John Mouledoux, Will Nagel, Thomas Parham, Heike Rau, Craig Reem, Liz Toomey and Kim Vater.

The UCI 50th anniversary committee, chaired by Vice Chancellor for Student Affairs Thomas Parham, also provided support. The committee comprises Daniel G. Aldrich III, Pam Brashear, Kelly Leanne Carland, Carolyn Canning-White, Ria Carlson, Justin Chung, Deborah Daniel, John Delshadi, Mark Deppe, Edgar Dormitorio, Angela Duby, Barney Ellis-Perry, Shannon Hartmeister, Paul Henisey, Janice Hopkins, Brice Ken Kikuchi, Herb Killackey, Kate Klimow, Julia R. Lupton, Richard Lynch, Sonali Madireddi, Sherry L. Main, James L. McGaugh, Leslie Millerd Rogers, Jeff Minhas, John Mouledoux, Will Nagel, Patrick Patterson, Robby Ray, Craig Reem, Donald Saari, Angela Simmons, Amanda Sivgals, Mitch Spann, Jessica Steward, Rameen Talesh, Jessica Terris, Liz Toomey, Victor Torres, Lisa Tran, Bayard Veiller, Zen Yieh and Audra Eagle Yun.

Colleagues in UC Irvine's Strategic Communications office pitched in with consistent good humor. Thanks to Steve Zylius, Will Nagel and Roberto Zepeda for assistance with photos and to Jennie Brewton, Janice Hopkins and Sherry Main for cover design ideas.

And finally the team at Third Millennium deserves our thanks. Editor Marina Dundjerski truly came to love and understand the traditions and pride points of UC Irvine and was dedicated to producing a quality publication. Photographer Julian Andrews' artistic eye beautifully captured the campus spirit. Designer Matthew Wilson worked patiently and tirelessly on cover ideas and page layouts. Sarah Yeatman helped with marketing and Neil Titman and Joel Burden provided the leadership that held it all together.

Thank you, all.

Cathy Lawhon
Senior director media relations and publications
50th Anniversary Committee

sponsors

This book has been made possible through the generosity of the following sponsors:

Julie Beth Abel, BA '01 Social Sciences

Kathleen Acab

Craig M. Adams, BA '74 Physical Sciences

Ramona H. Agrela, Staff

Jackie W. Alamo, BA '96 Social Sciences

Mark D. Alson, BS '86 Biological Sciences

Gina Amaro, BA '09 Social Ecology

Linda and Michael Arias, Staff / BA '11 Social Sciences

Jocelyn Arnold, BS '93 Biological Sciences; MBA '96 Paul Merage School of Business

Arthur Arrizon, BS '82 Engineering

Stewart Balikov DDS, BS '78 Biological Sciences

Keith Bangs, Staff

John Bauché, BA '05 Social Sciences

Rebecca Baugh, BA '73 Humanities

Marjorie Beale, Staff

Denis S. Bengin, BA '89 Social Sciences

Al Bennett, Professor of Biological Sciences

Jean Bennett, BA '05 Social Sciences

Rimal Bera, BS '83 Biological Sciences; MD '87 Medicine

Rudi Berkelhamer, Senior Lecturer, School of Biological Sciences

Dr Michael and Dr Ann Bernardo, BS '95 Biological Sciences / BS '95 Biological Sciences

Elizabeth Betowski, BA '03 Humanities

Scott Bollens

Breanna Joy Briggs, BA '15 Claire Trevor School of the Arts

Evan James Brock, BA '14 Social Sciences

Law Offices of Steven Jay Brock Inc.

Steven and Lillian Brock

Komal Broker, BA '12 Social Sciences

Brook Brown, BA '03 Humanities

Maria Hall Brown, BA '84 Claire Trevor School of the Arts

Kurt Busch, BS '93 Henry Samueli School of Engineering; BS '93 Biological Sciences

Camero Family

Raymond Camero, BS '95 Henry Samueli School of Engineering

Steve Capps, BA '69 Social Sciences

Ron Cargile

Ria Marie Carlson

Gabriel Castillo, BA '97 Social Ecology

Roy Y. Chan, BA '09 Social Ecology

Hseng-Hsin Christie Chang, MBA '98 Paul Merage School of Business

Robert Dale Chapman, BA '77 Physical Sciences; PhD '80 Physical Sciences

Nita L. Charlton, BA '90 Social Sciences

Prabir Chaudhury, PhD '88 Henry Samueli School of Engineering

William G. Cheadle MD, BA '76 Physical Sciences; BS '76 Biological Sciences; MD '80 Medicine

Jesse Y. Chen, BA '00 Humanities

Jiumn-Shiu Jason Chen, MBA '87 Paul Merage School of Business

Deric Chew, BA '13 Social Sciences

Carol Choi, BA '85 Social Sciences

Nigam Chokshi, BA '06 Social Sciences

Andrew Chou, BA '00 Social Sciences

Justin Chung, PhD '14 Information and Computer Sciences

Michael P. Clark, MA '73 Humanities; PhD '77 Humanities

Ralph and Carol Clayman, School of Medicine

Janet Shepherd Clifton, BA '70 Humanities; BA '70 Comparative Culture

Judith F. (Fabbri) Cobin, BA '89 Humanities

John E. Connolly MD FACS, Department of Surgery

Erkki W. Corpuz, BS '00 Biological Sciences

Richard J. Cote, BA '76 Physical Sciences; BA '76 Biological Sciences

Peter P. Cullen, MBPA '82 Administration

Tyler Cutforth, Researcher, Developmental and Cell Biology

Phi Dang, BS '03 Henry Samueli School of Engineering; MBA '12 Paul Merage School of Business
Deborah Daniel, BA '73 Humanities
Jeremy Matthew Davis, BS '74 Biological Sciences
Marc Davis, BS '94 Biological Sciences
James A. De Deo, BA '69 Humanities
Nick Desai, BS '91 Henry Samueli School of Engineering
Roman Diaz, Jr., BS '75 Information and Computer Science
Dennis Dierck, BA '01 Social Ecology
Ann Holland DiPlacito, BA '82 Social Ecology
Kimberly Donner, BS '09 Information and Computer Science
Juliet and Adam Dorn, BA '05 Social Sciences / BA '06 Social Ecology
Catherine E. Doyle, BA '12 Social Sciences
Professor Nikil Dutt, Donald Bren School of Information and Computer Sciences

Jacquelynne Eccles
Department of Ecology and Evolutionary Biology
Barney Ellis-Perry
Ronald D. Epperson, BS '69 Henry Samueli School of Engineering
Imelda Etemadieh
Amanda Evans, BS '10 Henry Samueli School of Engineering
Safali Patel Evans, BA '94 Social Sciences

David Fanous, BA '03 Social Sciences
Stephanie Fix, Staff
Kelly Lourdes Florimon
Chris and Danielle Fox, BS '93 Biological Sciences / BS '93 Biological Sciences
Anthony Frisbee, MAS '07 Social Ecology
Susan (Howard) Fritts, BA '76 Physical Sciences
Christina S. Frondoso, BA '95 Social Sciences
Edward S. Frondoso, BS '02 Henry Samueli School of Engineering

Jack F. Garate, BA '10 Humanities
Lauren Shigeko Gaskill, PhD '16 Humanities
Roberta and Max Geier, BA '82 Claire Trevor School of the Arts / BA '05 Social Sciences
Barbara Gyepes Giammona, BA '82 Humanities
Patricia Goheen, MFA '86 Claire Trevor School of the Arts
David Golbeck, BA '81 Claire Trevor School of the Arts
Kate Klimow Golbeck
Hal D. Goldflam, BA '92 Social Ecology
Kenneth Cho Gong, BS '80 Henry Samueli School of Engineering
Victor M. Gonzalez, MS '02 Information and Computer Science; PhD '06 Information and Computer Science
Gary Gorczyca, BA '73 Humanities
Barbara Berens Granger, BS '68 Biological Sciences; Staff '67–'00
Professor Gale (Morrie) Granger, Staff '67–'02
Jean M. Granger, PhD '86 Social Ecology
James D. Green, Jr., BA '07 Social Sciences
Neel Grover, BA '92 Social Sciences
Erin Gruwell, BA '91 Humanities
Bobby and Shelley Gupta, BS '92 Biological Sciences; BS '92 Physical Sciences / BS '92 Biological Sciences
Gary Guymon

Harry Hansen, BA '77 Information and Computer Science
Michael B. Harrington, MS '69 Paul Merage School of Business; PhD '73 Paul Merage School of Business
Elizabeth Farotte Heenan, BA '03 Claire Trevor School of the Arts
Paul Henisey
John Herklotz
Harry W. Herr MD, MD '69 Medicine
Brian Hill, BA '91 Social Sciences
Chris Hillock, EMBA '15 Paul Merage School of Business
Kathy Hills, BS '83 Biological Sciences
S.J. and Raul Hinojosa, Jr., Staff
Nobuko Jane Hiramine, BA '99 Social Ecology
Samuel Y. Ho, BA '07 Social Sciences
Susan Y. Ho, BA '08 Social Sciences
Hollencrest Capital Mgmt
Jeremy Horne, BS '12 Henry Samueli School of Engineering
J. DeWayne and Lisa Houck-Green, BS '76 Biological Sciences; MBA '91 Paul Merage School of Business / BS '76 Biological Sciences
Gerard and Barbara Van Hoven, Emeriti
Henry Y. Huang, BA '97 Social Sciences
Thomas C. Huang, BS '82 Biological Sciences
John Hung, BS '89 Information and Computer Science; BA '90 Social Sciences

Cosmin Ibanescu, MBA '07 Paul Merage School of Business
Florante and Rose Ibanez, BA '77 Comparative Culture
City of Irvine

Jenny and Drew Jedlinsky, BA '03 Humanities / BA '03 Social Sciences
Victor C. Joe
Ruth Walton Johnson, PhD '73 Biological Sciences
Kim R. (Kleve) Jones, BA '83 Social Sciences
Steven and Elaine Jong, BS '99 Biological Sciences; BA '99 Social Sciences / BA '98 Social Ecology

Lynn Kaplan-Stevens, BA '89 Social Ecology
Tim Kashani, BS '86 Information and Computer Science; MBA '88 Paul Merage School of Business
Kate Kassuba, Staff
Allen Katouli, BS '03 Physical Sciences; MS '05 Physical Sciences; PhD '09 Physical Sciences
Glen Kauffman, BS '86 Information and Computer Science; MBA '94 Paul Merage School of Business
Terrance M. Keen, BA '72 Social Sciences; BS '72 Information and Computer Sciences
Claudia Bonilla Keller, BA '87 Social Sciences
Timothy S. Kelly
Richard Kikuchi, BA '89 Social Sciences
Elaine Y. King MD, BS '95 Biological Sciences; MD '99 Medicine
Samuel J. King, MBA '00 Paul Merage School of Business
Dagmar Klaus
Deborah Kloman, BA '85 Social Sciences; MBA '87 Paul Merage School of Business
Jesse Knepper, BA '96 Social Sciences
Janet Knutsen, BA '75 Humanities; BA '75 Comparative Culture
John Kramer, BS '69 Henry Samueli School of Engineering
Peter Krapp

Joseph Lara, BS '78 Biological Sciences
Lucia Veronica (Morici) Larkin, BA '04 Social Ecology

Richard H. Lathrop, Professor of Computer Science

Peter T. Le, BA '91 Social Sciences

Harry and Denise Le Grande, BA '75 Social Ecology

Susan Diane Lear, BA '73 Humanities

David Wah-Fai Lee, BMUS '03 Claire Trevor School of the Arts; MBA '12 Paul Merage School of Business

Kenneth Y. Lee, BS '92 Henry Samueli School of Engineering; MS '95 Henry Samueli School of Engineering; PhD '99 Henry Samueli School of Engineering

Sandy Nga Lee, BA '99 Social Sciences

William Lee, MD '62 Medicine

Gregory R. Leet and Albie J. Micklich DMA

Carl Lenhart, BA '70 Humanities

David and Diana (Ma) Lieu, MD '79 Medicine / BS '79 Biological Sciences

Ilya and Elizaveta Litvak, MS '05 Physical Sciences; PhD '10 Physical Sciences / MS '10 Physical Sciences; PhD '13 Physical Sciences

Olga and Mikhail Litvak

Jeff Juqiang Liu, MS '99 Henry Samueli School of Engineering; PhD '02 Henry Samueli School of Engineering

Nancy Locke, Staff

Adam Lokeh MD, BS '90 Biological Sciences

Krystal Rose Lopez, MAS '13 Social Ecology

David P. Love, BA '71 Physical Sciences; MA '73 Physical Sciences; PhD '78 Physical Sciences

Vonessa Low, BA '11 Social Ecology

Ravy Lu, BS '89 Biological Sciences

Julia Reinhard Lupton, Professor, School of Humanities

Geisce Ly, BA '96 Social Ecology

Rich and Doris Lynch, Staff

Lawrence E. Maddox, BA '91 Social Sciences

Sivan Mahadevan, BS '85 Information and Computer Science

Sherry and Paul Main, MBA '09 Paul Merage School of Business / BS '00 Henry Samueli School of Engineering; MS '07 Information and Computer Science

Mirela Manea-Krichten, MS '86 Physical Sciences; PhD '91 Physical Sciences

Andrew Markis

Lydia E. Martinez Campos, MFA '00 Claire Trevor School of the Arts

Toni Martinovich, BA '80 Claire Trevor School of the Arts

Richard L. Masserman MD, MD '65 Medicine

Goran Matijasevic, MS '85 Henry Samueli School of Engineering; PhD '91 Henry Samueli School of Engineering

Gary and Maya Matkin

Caitlin Knutsen McCann, BA '10 Humanities

Gail Munro McClain, BA '67 Humanities

John E. McCue, BA '68 Humanities

Scott McGarrigle, BS '87 Physical Sciences

Gary McQuarrie, BS '75 Biological Sciences; BS '75 Physical Sciences

Rudy Medina MD, BS '84 Biological Sciences

Perry Ian Melnick, BA '03 Social Sciences

Jason Merchey, BA '97 Social Ecology

Douglas Merrill

Metherate Family

Kathryn Adella Riley Miller, BA '82 Humanities

Sandra Milligan, BS '86 Biological Sciences; BA '86 Social Sciences

Jeff and Maggie Minhas, BA '04 Social Sciences / BA '05 Social Ecology

Jason Montgomery, BA '12 Social Sciences

Daniel and Kelly Montplaisir

Thomas Moore, BA '78 Humanities

Dan Morgan, BS '10 Information and Computer Science

Professor D.R. Mumm

Peggy Munhall, BA Social Ecology '78; Staff

Vilas H. Munshi, MS '69 Henry Samueli School of Engineering

Ajanta Naidu MD, MBA '11 Paul Merage School of Business

Ronak Mahesh Naik, BS '11 Henry Samueli School of Engineering

Susan Nakamura, BA '82 Claire Trevor School of the Arts

Pittawat Narktawan, MS '12 Program in Nursing Science

Fred Niditch, MA '74 Humanities

Beverly Sigler Noble, BA '70 Social Sciences

The Program in Nursing Science

Evangeline Rustia Obrero PA-C, BS '95 Biological Sciences

David Ochi, BA '97 Social Sciences; BS '97 Biological Sciences; MBA '99 Paul Merage School of Business

Gregg Oelker, BS '77 Biological Sciences; BS '77 Physical Sciences

Gary and Judy Olson

Cynthia Mari Orozco, BA '05 Social Sciences

Kelly Lee Oto, BA '95 Social Ecology

Bradford Jon Ottoson, BS '78 Information and Computer Science

Karen Lynn Malone Ottoson, BA '77 Social Ecology

Toni McDonald Pang

Gerald Parham, BA '77 Social Ecology

Vice Chancellor Thomas Anthony Parham, BA '77 Social Ecology

Mark Passarini, BS '77 Henry Samueli School of Engineering

Victor Passy, MD '62 Medicine

Gary Perez, BA '86 Social Sciences

Cynthia Van Name Peters, BA '78 Social Ecology

Kevin H. Phung, BS '12 Biological Sciences; BA '12 Social Sciences

Jessica Pratt, PhD '13 Biological Sciences

Judith L. Puritz, MBA '03 Paul Merage School of Business

Manette Quinn, MBA '06 Paul Merage School of Business

James H. Quon, BA '00 Social Sciences

Singha Rakyong, BS '14 Information and Computer Science

Teri Lombardo Ramirez, BA '99 Social Sciences

Craig Reem

Claudia V. Renteria

Stacey Richardson, BA '81 Social Sciences

Robert G. Rodriguez, BA '94 Social Sciences

Helmut R. Roessler, MA '68 Humanities

Robert Romney, MS '83 Information and Computer Science

Jose Romo-Velazquez, BA '15 Information and Computer Science

Brian Roode

J. Alex Rubio, MBA '15 Paul Merage School of Business

Pamela Rust

Tania Hadeel Saba, BA '06 Humanities

Fred Sainick, BA '74 Humanities

Adrian Salamanca, BA '05 Social Sciences

J.M. Ian Salas, PhD '13 Social Sciences

Sean M. Sampson, BS '09 Program In Nursing Science

Beverly "Babs" Sandeen, BA '84 Social Sciences; PhD '97 Social Ecology

Stephen Sandis, JD '12 Law

Devin Schirm, BA '14 Social Sciences

Matthew Thomas Schweiger

Deborah-Lore C. Secard, BA '76 Social Ecology

Mike Segawa, BA '79 Social Sciences

Timothy Milton Seiler, BA '86 Social Sciences

Ed Semblantes, Staff

Marilyn Shaw, BA '82 Social Ecology

Pamela Jane Sheldon, BA '72 Humanities

Edmond Shi, BS '83 Information and Computer Science; MBA '86 Paul Merage School of Business; MS '91 Information and Computer Science

Alvin C. Shon MD, BS '75 Biological Sciences

Lisa Shoup, BA '81 Humanities

Kelsey Marie Skaggs, BA '12 Social Sciences

Steven L. Small, Professor and Chair, Neurology School of Medicine

Donna Brich Smith, BA '81 Humanities; MA '82 Humanities

Erik Smith, BA '14 Claire Trevor School of the Arts

Kyle Smith, BA '04 Social Sciences

Thomas D. Smith, BA '08 Social Ecology; BA '08 Social Sciences

School of Social Ecology

Mitchell and Maureen Spann, Staff

Michael J. Stamos MD, Chair, Department of Surgery

Roger F. Steinert MD, Chair, Department of Ophthalmology

James W. Stewart, BS '69 Henry Samueli School of Engineering

Michael and Della Stewart, BA '87 Social Sciences / BA '88 Claire Trevor School of the Arts; BA '88 Social Sciences

John Stupar, Lecturer, School of Engineering

James Sullivant, BS '76 Biological Sciences

Donna Augustine Symons, BA '69 Humanities

Paul M. Takeshita, BS '75 Biological Sciences

Rameen Talesh, BA '89 Social Sciences

Diana Dresser Tallie, BA '77 Humanities

John Tang and Family, BS '94 Biological Sciences

Rebecca Tangen

Lorelei Tanji, Staff

Virginia (Tucker) Thomas, BA '69 Social Sciences

Ann McNaughton Thompson, BA '67 Claire Trevor School of the Arts; MFA '71 Claire Trevor School of the Arts

Jack Toan, BS '96 School of Biological Sciences; MBA '02 Paul Merage School of Business

Jason and Armi Tompkins, BA '00 Social Sciences / BA '02 Claire Trevor School of the Arts

James D. Tran, BA '00 Social Ecology

John Turner, Assistant Professor, Paul Merage School of Business

UCI Office of Research

William T. Um, BA '90 Social Sciences

Office of the University Registrar

Jason Valdry, BS '98 Information and Computer Science; MBA '08 Paul Merage School of Business

Rick Van Etten MD PhD, Director, Chao Family Comprehensive Cancer Center

Deborah and Kerry Vandell, Faculty, School of Education and School of Business

Victor H. Velasquez, BS '01 Physical Sciences

Chuck Villanueva, BS '93 Biological Sciences

Brenda Renee Villegas, BA '01 Social Ecology

Dinah M. Viloria, MBA '90 Paul Merage School of Business

Wilima Wadhwa, MA '89 Social Sciences; PhD '90 Social Sciences

John Wallace, BS '78 Physical Sciences; BS '78 Biological Sciences

Biying Wang

William Waterhouse, BA '69 Social Sciences

James Weatherall, PhD '12 Social Sciences

Office of the Assistant Vice Chancellor for Wellness, Health and Counseling Services

Douglas Whipple MD, BS '86 Biological Sciences

Claudia White, BA '89 Social Sciences

Steven A. White, BA '69 Physical Sciences

Barbara Whitney, BA '77 Claire Trevor School of the Arts

Shellyanne Sealy Wilder, BS '95 Physical Sciences

Ann Williams, Staff

Kathleen Pickett Willman, BS '83 Physical Sciences

Christina (Frank) Wilson, BA '99 Social Ecology

Dr Garrett Wirth, Associate Clinical Professor, School of Medicine

Donald Wong, BS '14 Biological Sciences

Kathryn L. Wong, BMUS '97 Claire Trevor School of the Arts

Kristi Wong

Michelle Yuen Ting Wong, BA '12 Social Sciences

James E. Wood, Jr., MD '73 Medicine

Harry Woolway, BA '89 Social Ecology

Wayne Wu, BS '12 Henry Samueli School of Engineering

Lawrence J. Wysocki, BS '75 Biological Sciences

Kaikai Xu, PhD '14 Henry Samueli School of Engineering

Jack and Kimberly Yang, BA '06 Social Sciences / BA '05 Humanities

Audra Eagle Yun, Staff

UC Irvine would also like the thank the following for their continued support:

Alicia W. ('76) and David A. Abell

Linda and Richard C. Ackerman

Allergan, Inc.

Alzheimer's Association of Orange County, Inc.

American Cancer Society Inc.

American Diabetes Association

American Heart Association

Analytical Graphics, Inc.

Archstone Foundation

Julia and George L. Argyros

AWR Corporation

Hana and Francisco J. Ayala

Judith D. and Dennis J. Baker ('79)

Peter J. Balsells, Sr.

Bausch & Lomb

The Beall Family

Arnold and Mabel Beckman Foundation

Beckman Laser Institute

Nancy E. and Gary H. Beverage

The Boeing Company

Penelope and D'Arcy Bolton

Magdalena and Amer A. Boukai ('85)

The Breast Cancer Research Foundation

Brigitte and Donald Bren

The Donald Bren Foundation

Susan M. and Richard K. Bridgford

Jane Buchan and James A. Driscoll

Audrey S. Burnand

Paul E. and Katherine Jo Butterworth

Karen J. and Bruce E. Cahill

California Community Foundation, Inc.

Carnegie Corporation of New York

California Institute for Regenerative Medicine

Esther M. and James H. Cavanaugh
Allen and Lee-Hwa Chao
June T. and Richard Y. Chao
Salma A. ('99) and Hazem H. Chehabi
Lorna L. ('69) and Robert S. Cohen
Conexant
Discovery Eye Foundation
Priscilla A. and Ranney E. Draper
Doris Duke Charitable Foundation
Diane M. and Joseph L. Dunn
Sandra J. and Dale L. Dykema
Edison International
Ellison Medical Foundation
Emulex Corporation
Ruth A. and John R. Evans
Experian
Awilda and Robert R. Fagin
Dina and Jean-Claude Falmagne
The Fletcher Jones Foundation
The Ford Foundation
Foundation for the National Institutes of Health, Inc.
Lynn and Douglas Freeman
Edwin D. Fuller
Melinda F. and William H. Gates, III
Monica L. and David Gelbaum ('72)
John D. ('87) and Evelyn ('88) Gerace
Janet and James C. Gianulias
William J. Gillespie
Josephine D. Gleis
Google, Inc.
Sue and Bill Gross
Emile and Dina Haddad
Merry E. and John S. Hagestad
Bernadette and Raouf Halim
Bruce R. ('78) and Elizabeth M. Hallett
John A. Hartford Foundation
Lynette and Michael K. Hayde
Hellman Fellows Fund
The Henry Luce Foundation
Ninetta K. and Gavin S. Herbert, Sr.
Julie and Peter J. Hill
Larry L. Hillblom Foundation Inc.
Phylis and David C. Hsia
Howard Hughes Medical Institute
Gary H. Hunt
Irvine Health Foundation

Catherine T. and Frank Jao
Robert Wood Johnson Foundation
Juvenile Diabetes Research Foundation International
Helen and Steeve T. Kay
W.M. Keck Foundation
Anne L. and Rick E. Keller, Jr.
Sidney and Granville Kirkup
Jenny B. ('78) and William G. Klein
Barbara L. and Robert A. Kleist
Beth L. Koehler
Susan G. Komen Foundation
Richard P. Kratz
Agnes Y. and Jen K. Kung
Jack and Shanaz Langson
Marsha D. and William J. Link
Elizabeth F. Loftus
John S. and Marilyn Long
John and Catherine MacArthur Foundation
Josiah Macy Foundation
Rana and Mohannad S. Malas
March of Dimes Birth Defects Foundation
Marisla Foundation
Twyla R. and Charles D. Martin
Azam and Dr. Fariborz Maseeh
Geneva M. Matlock
Keleen B. and James Mazzo
The Andrew W. Mellon Foundation
Elisabeth F. and Paul Merage
Ruth M. and Roger J. Miller
Barbara F. and Roscoe H. Moore, Jr.
The Gordon and Betty Moore Foundation
Charles Stewart Mott Foundation
MSC Software Corporation
Muscular Dystrophy Association
Linda J. and Michael A. Mussallem
National Math + Science Initiative, Inc.
National Multiple Sclerosis Society
Lila D. and Eric L. Nelson
Martha A. (PhD '81) and James A. Newkirk
Dennis L. Nguyen ('94)
The Nicholas Endowment
Henry T. Nicholas, III
Stacey Nicholas
Marilyn and Thomas H. Nielsen
Opus Foundation

Orange County Community Foundation
Orange County United Way
Bernard Osher Foundation
Pediatrix Medical Group, Inc.
The William Lion Penzner Foundation
Sheila and James J. Peterson
The Podlich Family
Mark Porterfield (MBA '85)
Raymond Pryke
Jeffrey M. Rehm and Stuart A. Byer
Donald W. Reynolds Foundation
Melody and Mark P. Robinson, Jr.
Michelle F. Rohe
The Rose Hills Foundation
Russell Sage Foundation
Cheryll R. and Richard J. Ruszat
Susan F. and Henry Samueli
Kathleen R. and Mark K. Santora
Audrey M. Schneiderman
Sherry F. ('79) and Michael Schulman
Helen Shanbrom
Shur-Lok Corporation
Simons Foundation
Melanie C. and Gary J. Singer ('74)
Branna E. Sisenwein
Alfred P. Sloan Foundation
Janice F. and Ted Smith
Joan Irvine Smith
Margaret L. Sprague
Suzanne L. and Ralph Stern
Sandra and David Stone
Madeline M. and James I. Swinden
John Templeton Foundation
Nancy E. and William S. Thompson, Jr.
Edward Thorp
Elizabeth C. and Thomas T. Tierney
Toyota Motor Sales, U.S.A., Inc.
Janie and Victor Tsao
Betty K. Tu ('99) and David L. Tsoong
Mary W. and John Tu
UniHealth Foundation
Jean B. and Timothy W. Weiss
Whitehall Foundation, Inc.
Shiou-Jin C. and James T. Yang
Mei C. and Dean A. Yoost
Misako and Thomas C. Yuen ('74)